Do-It-Yourself Retirement

Can I Retire Yet?

How to Make
the Biggest Financial Decision
of the Rest of Your Life

Darrow Kirkpatrick

StructureByDesign
Chattanooga, Tennessee 37405

ISBN: 978-0-9892830-2-1

www.CanIRetireYet.com

Dedication

To those who question…

Disclaimer

The content here contains personal opinions of the author regarding financial and economic matters. It is for educational purposes only. The publisher and author do not imply or intend any guarantee of accuracy. The information here is not necessarily suitable for every individual: Use it at your own risk. No guarantees are made that you will achieve results similar to those described here, or any specific results whatsoever from using the concepts and approaches discussed. No guarantees are implied or expressed. Though reasonable effort has been taken to make this material as useful as possible, there may be typographical mistakes or errors in the content. Neither the author nor the publisher is engaged in rendering professional services including, but not limited to, accounting, tax, legal, or investment planning. This information is not intended as a substitute for such professional services. If specific advice is needed or appropriate, the reader should seek out and engage a licensed professional. The author and publisher specifically disclaim any liability, loss, or risk taken by readers who directly or indirectly act on this information. You are solely responsible for your own decisions and actions, and their results.

Contents

INTRODUCTION

"In preparing for battle I have always found that plans are useless, but planning is indispensable." — General Dwight D. Eisenhower

You've worked a long time. You may have lived frugally, saved diligently, paid for college, paid off the house. Your investments are doing well, and the markets seem relatively stable, for now. You've amassed more assets than you dreamed possible, and yet you hesitate. ***"Will it be enough?"***

You run retirement calculators and solicit opinions. Some financial advisors say you need millions. Others who've done it say you should quit earlier, while you still have your health and can enjoy life. You analyze and ponder, *but you still can't seem to make the retirement decision.* So you keep working, hoping that more money will guarantee a secure retirement, and more time will make the decision easier. Another year passes, and it's the same story....

Could this be you? It's a familiar story in discussions I have with readers and others. There is a lack of certainty around the retirement equation for everyone. Just how much do you need? If you have a steady pension, or many millions, then you can retire with few worries. But the vast majority of us will never know with absolute certainty that we have enough money set aside. Sure, you can pay a financial planner to crunch your numbers and create some fancy reports with reassuring-looking graphs. And, after a few years, if that long, events will take a different course and you'll realize it was all pure *speculation*.

An old television commercial showed prospective retirees going about their daily tasks with their "number" (the amount they needed to save in order to retire) hovering over their heads. While there is nothing wrong with having a specific target, just don't put too much stock in it. The future is far too uncertain over the 30- to 40-year time span of a modern retirement to believe that there is a static number or system that will keep you safe and secure for every possible outcome.

Yet the question lingers: *Can I retire yet?*

I faced that puzzle some time ago, managed to solve it, and left my secure career behind with confidence. Did I figure out precisely how much money I needed to safely retire? *No*. Because, as I will explain later, that is technically impossible. But I did make peace with a reasonable answer, decided to retire, and have no regrets today, years later. You can too.

Paradoxically, the question *"How much is enough to retire?"* may not have an exact answer. But, the question *"Am I well enough prepared for the future that I can leave my full-time job?"* is one that does. The math may be indefinite, but you can still make a definite decision....

This book is about that decision as much as it is about an answer. It's about how *I* made that decision, and what I've learned since. During the accumulation years, and now as an early retiree, I learned to focus on the current *reality* –

knowing exactly where you are and what forces are in play. Then you can take the best possible action for your current stage in life, and the years that will follow.

Whether you are retiring early, or at a more traditional age, *the future remains uncertain*. Very few of the baby boomers or succeeding generations will achieve the level of wealth needed to banish every possible financial concern in retirement. But many of us – those who have worked hard, lived prudently, and prepared diligently – *will* have the tools necessary to be comfortable and secure for the rest of our lives.

In my experience, retirement is a *gateway*, not a destination. The retirement years can potentially be the most fulfilling period of your life. By planning in advance as best you can, starting prepared, and making the most of whatever comes, you can ensure those years will be the best possible!

Overview

The chapters that follow show how to assess your retirement expenses and income, as well as navigate your way through the retirement years, without needing to fully predict the future. I'll be presenting research to reinforce key points, and offering rules of thumb to organize and streamline the process as much as possible. There are no absolute answers. But there are wise *behaviors* to employ, including, among others, diversification, prudence, and flexibility.

This book is for anyone who intends to pilot his or her own ship during retirement. Doing retirement planning and money management *yourself* is usually the surest way to maintain your financial independence, because it costs less, and is tuned to your own needs and capabilities. Your nest egg represents your accumulated life energy, and your future freedom. In most cases, there is no one who can exercise the same care and wisdom with your wealth that *you* can. So, I strongly encourage you not to relinquish the key decision-making for your money.

We are about to explore all the most relevant issues and factors in trying to answer the question *"Can I Retire Yet?"*

The book is divided into five main sections. In the first section we size up your retirement *expenses* – the first half of the fundamental retirement equation. We consider whether you've dispensed with, or prepared for, various major life expenses, and then analyze how much it will cost you to live in retirement. Finally, we investigate three potentially serious threats to your retirement lifestyle: health care cost and availability, inflation, and taxes.

In the second section we turn to your retirement *income*, which must cover those retirement expenses. We briefly touch on pensions, which a diminishing few of us will enjoy. Then we turn to Social Security – which will be an essential income stream for most modern retirees. Can you count on it and, if so, how much? Next, we review your life savings or investment portfolio, which must be able to fill in any gaps in the previously considered income, by generating dividends and growth. We also review the philosophical and practical differences between relying on stock market probabilities via an investment portfolio versus "safer" insurance products for retirement income. We discuss how to create a "guaranteed" lifetime income stream using an annuity. Finally, we consider how to integrate these income streams and supplement them by working part-time in retirement – a financial and emotional necessity for many.

In sections three and four we turn to the most difficult topic in the book, the one on which countless pages have been written and for which millions in advising fees have been charged: *predicting the future*. In essence, that is what most attempts at retirement planning are all about. We begin with a primer on the retirement equation and retirement calculators. We analyze just how uncertain retirement predictions are, and discuss if and when it makes sense to pay somebody else for financial advice. We review the major inputs to the retirement calculation, along with tips for making it more accurate. Then we delve into the concept of a "safe" withdrawal rate, which has been the traditional approach to living off a portfolio, and the new wave of research raising questions about how safe that really is. Then we get as close as humanly possible to answering the retirement number question, by bracketing the envelope of realistic withdrawal rate possibilities. That leads to a frank assessment of *your* actual withdrawal rate. How comfortable will you be traveling through retirement? Will you be *walking* (short on necessities), *driving* (cautiously comfortable), or *cruising* (no money concerns)?

Finally, in the fifth section of the book, we'll integrate the previous chapters and apply that knowledge to managing your money and navigating your retirement journey as it unfolds. We'll start by helping you assess the economic conditions at your retirement date – a key indicator for retirement success, and the potential performance of your portfolio. Next, we'll discuss how you can safely generate cash flow from your assets to meet your expenses in retirement. We'll discuss how to track your financial condition as retirement progresses, and we'll deal frankly with the very real concern of running out of money in retirement, including what to do if it begins to look like you won't have enough. To ease those concerns, we'll discuss your options for realistic *lifeboat strategies* that can ensure you are never without the basic living essentials.

We'll conclude with a complete but simple strategy for making the retirement decision and leaving work, plus some personal thoughts on life in retirement.

The book is organized to map out the mental terrain that I believe most real-world, do-it-yourself retirees must traverse. You begin by understanding your personal inputs to the *retirement equation* – your expenses, and income. You then dig deeper into that equation, understanding the relationship between income and assets in retirement. You learn how to analyze that relationship using the best available retirement calculators. Reviewing their output, you understand the prospects for predicting the future. Finally, given the difficulties in actually knowing that future, you develop a toolbox for dealing with whatever comes. And, in refining that toolbox, you find the confidence to make the retirement decision. *That was my experience, and I believe it can be yours too.*

Note: for any late-breaking corrections or additions to the book, plus a list of web addresses corresponding to hyperlinks appearing on the following pages, please visit this page on my web site:

www.caniretireyet.com/book2/

My Background

I grew up in a Navy family where I learned integrity, economy, and the value of work. I'm an Eagle Scout, and graduated with a degree in Civil Engineering from the University of Virginia. Soon after college I discovered personal computers, and got in on the ground floor of the PC revolution.

I started my own software company, which I eventually sold to a pioneer in numerical modeling for PCs. That company sold to a global leader in architecture and engineering software. I retired from that company in the spring of 2011 after 29 years of programming, designing, and managing computer software.

I began serious saving and investing in my mid-30's. I was 50 when I retired, financially independent, with a net worth over $1 million, owning our house free and clear, with no debt of any kind.

I'm not a dot-com or Silicon Valley type of millionaire. I also didn't become financially independent by flipping real estate or trading hot stocks. Over many years, I did it the traditional way: hard work, frugality, careful investing, and patience.

I'm an engineer, not a salesperson or a financial advisor. When it comes to money, my top priorities are simplicity, safety, and reliability. Now my mission is to help others live well and become financially independent as I did, through my writing about personal finance.

My blog *Can I Retire Yet?* receives tens of thousands of visitors each month and has been quoted in *Consumer Reports*, *Money Magazine*, *The Huffington Post*, *The Wall Street Journal*, and many other publications.

My Decision

An essential prerequisite for retiring is first having time to study and plan for the future. As a working engineer, I learned and studied the retirement equation and made my retirement decision over a period of years. During that time, I looked at retirement cash flow in a number of different ways:

I started with my own analysis, using basic engineering economics. Then I ran my numbers through a dozen retirement calculators from some of the biggest names in financial services. In the process, I learned a lot about how the retirement equation is modeled. The results were mixed, to say the least! *I was shocked by the variation and outright errors in the answers.* Some calculators crashed or gave nonsense results. The others, while generally confirming my ability to retire, produced widely varying answers – a range of about $8 million in ending portfolio values!

Though I felt generally confident about retiring early, there was some lingering uncertainty. I knew a lot about this topic from studying it over the years, but I found myself wanting a second opinion. Ironically, I didn't turn to my financial institutions to help with this critical decision. Frankly, I didn't consider them impartial, or expert: How vested were they in my achieving financial freedom? *How many of those advisors had actually managed to leave their jobs to retire early?*

I wanted second opinions from individuals who had *lived* the topic – through their writing, or life, preferably both. But there were very few personal finance books focused on the retirement question from a first-person perspective. So I went online, to the world of personal finance blogs. I felt certain that somebody who was already financially independent, or somebody with the confidence to pull the plug on a secure job, would be in a much better position to help me make an informed, impartial decision. And I knew they would have no agenda, other than helping me to find the correct answer.

In blogs such as *Early Retirement Extreme*, *Financial Mentor*, *Oblivious Investor*, and *Mr. Money Mustache*, and their associated books, I found the confirmation I needed, as well as my future passion.

Early vs. Traditional Retirement

Before we dive into how to determine your own retirement equation, we should clarify a critical distinction that will divide readers of this book into two groups: Are you an *early* or *traditional* retiree? This book is for both, but bear in mind that since it was written by an *early* retiree, I will generally be taking that perspective unless noted otherwise.

"Retirement" is a slippery concept. That *R-word* is commonly used, and that's why I use it here and on my blog. But it can describe radically different situations: a 20-something Internet tycoon; an extremely frugal 30-something software engineer; a 40-something ex-military officer on a pension; a 50-something engineer who achieved financial independence with prudent investing; or a 60-something on Social Security. They might all be considered "retired."

The conventional definition of retirement is to *stop working*, to "withdraw from one's occupation." But when I use the word "retirement," especially *early retirement* – in your 50's or earlier – what I really mean is "a level of financial independence that allows foregoing the security of a full-time job." That means having the freedom to live life at your own speed, being creative and productive on your own terms. And, for many of us, that will still lead to something that looks, at least occasionally, like "*work*."

In my experience, there are two distinct classes of retirement: *early* retirement and *traditional* retirement. There is no official definition, but the following table of relevant factors might help clarify what I mean by those terms, and where *you* fit into the picture:

Table: Early vs. Traditional Retirement

Retirement	Age	Length	Pension	Health Insurance	Could work?
Early	50's or younger	40+ years	no	purchased	yes
Traditional	60's+	20-30 years	yes	Medicare/benefit	no

Of these factors, one stands out as a fundamental dividing line, with critical implications for the retirement equation: Are you willing and able to return to some enjoyable, part-time *work* if needed? That option can substitute for a great deal of savings, and it can prevent a great deal of anxiety and over-preparation for certain scenarios that could lead to running out of money in retirement.

Given the uncertainties around modern retirement, unless you've saved a great deal of money (we'll discuss just how much in section 4), it's probably irresponsible to leave a career for early retirement, unless you have the option to work again if things don't go well. The range of possible investment returns, inflation rates, and health care costs over the long time spans involved in early retirement, magnify the already unknowable variables in most retirement equations.

The ability and desire to *work*, in some capacity, is a hallmark of early retirees. However, it might not even be an option for the traditional retiree.

So, where exactly is that dividing line for you? Personally, I see my 60's as a point where I would in no way want to be *forced* to return to work. Before that, I'm willing to work, if certain dire economic scenarios were to take shape. It would not be a catastrophe in my life and could even be fun and rewarding.

In fact, I've continued *working* on my blog and related projects, in early retirement. I might have withdrawn from my original career, but I'm not at all withdrawn from the productive world. However, I do this "work" on my own terms, at my own speed. And it's not primarily about money: Financial considerations take a back seat to quality of life.

Your Decision

Your situation could very well be different from mine. You might have complicating personal, family, or financial factors. Or you may not have the technical background or financial experience to confidently assess your own retirement. As much as I believe in do-it-yourself retirement, and as hard as I will work to give you the tools for that in this book, this is simply too important a decision to risk if you are anything less than completely confident.

So, if, in your opinion, you need a trusted financial advisor to make this decision, then by all means get one. (I'll offer a few tips on choosing an advisor later in the book.)

Also understand that some of what I have to say is influenced by my perspective as an *early retiree,* one who has *taken calculated risks – both personally and professionally – his entire life.* I retired at an age, and with a technical skill set, where it would be feasible (though not easy) for me to return to an income-producing career, if absolutely required.

On the other side of the equation, my wife and I have camped, climbed, biked, and traveled extensively all over the world in all kinds of conditions. After retirement, we could have lived happily out of our RV or a small cottage for a while, if we needed to reduce our expenses.

These are options that may not exist for you if retiring in your 60's or later, with health issues, or certain lifestyle requirements. *Use your own judgment about what is best for you.*

Don't expect to do everything the way I did. And, if you do, don't expect to get the same results, necessarily. We all walk our own path, subject to our own history. Some of us will decide to retire earlier, with the attendant risks of running out of money. Others will decide to work longer, with the attendant risks of running out of *life*.

But, if you'll select from among the tested ideas in this book the ones that make sense to you, and apply them to suit your own situation, then you'll be much better prepared for a successful retirement.

I believe the lessons I've learned in making the retirement decision will help speed and improve your own journey. Like each of life's major decisions, this one is part logic, part emotion, and part leap of faith. *Best wishes on your transition to what's next!*

Backup Plans

The older you are, the shorter your retirement and the more *predictable* your retirement planning can be. A 20-year traditional retirement is a very different scenario from a 40+ year early retirement. Anyone who has spent much time with a retirement calculator can attest: results begin to diverge dramatically as the decades add on.

Because of the decades-long time spans involved, and the unknowability of future events, a key component of any retirement, in my opinion, is having a **backup plan.** The essence of such a backup plan is having the ability to either *cut your expenses* or *raise your income*, if required.

Early retirees especially need such a plan, and usually have more flexibility to create one. They can often implement a plan on the *expense* side of the equation – cutting living expenses in one or more categories, for example. Younger retirees are more likely to be spending on travel or other recreation that could be cut back. And they are more likely to have options for moving to a cheaper location or into a downsized home that could substantially cut their cost of living. We'll discuss these options further in section 5 of the book.

Even traditional retirees have options available for a backup plan, particularly on the *income* side of the equation. Some of the most common choices for those traditional retirees include annuitizing assets to create a higher income stream, or taking out a reverse mortgage to generate lifetime income from home equity. We'll also discuss these details in section 5.

Work, at least part-time, serves as the preferred backup plan for many early retirees. Working would likely impact their preferred lifestyle less than other options. If that's the case for you, then you must consider two factors before taking the plunge into retirement: (1) How marketable will your skills be in the future economy? (2) How plentiful will relevant jobs be at precisely the time you are likely to need to shore up your retirement finances – possibly during a major, extended recession?

Given those questions, early retirees who hope to enjoy living for many more decades need to guard their *personal productivity* more carefully than traditional retirees. If you're a younger retiree, you should maintain your professional contacts, or develop new ones. You should stay informed about advancements in your chosen field, or develop experience in another area that interests you. And you should always be on the lookout for easy and fun ways to be of service or to create value for others.

In my experience, if you are a competent and informed *early* retiree who enjoys helping others, you will never want for ways to produce income, if necessary. The *traditional* retiree, of which there will be fewer and fewer in the future, does not usually need to be concerned with such matters....

1: SIZING UP YOUR RETIREMENT EXPENSES

"You can have anything you want, you just can't have everything you want." — Williams/Jeppson/Botkin, *Money*

"Gain may be temporary and uncertain; but ever while you live, expense is constant and certain..." — Benjamin Franklin

In this section, we'll get into detailed planning for what daily living is likely to cost you in retirement. And we'll also consider three of the potentially most serious threats to a comfortable retirement – health care costs, inflation, and taxes.

When you're done with this section, you'll have a feel for the cost of living in retirement. You'll know the major budget categories you must plan for. And you'll have a sense of what those categories are costing others in retirement. Finally, you'll also appreciate those variables that defy prediction.

To get started, let's dispense with a handful of major deal-killers that could derail your retirement before it ever gets off the ground....

Are the Major Life Expenses Behind You?

Here are three major expenses that most potential retirees will want in their rearview mirror before leaving a secure job: college education for their kids, mortgages, and consumer debt. There may be exceptional situations where people retire while still managing these expenses in their lives, but it's rare.

College

Seeing one or more children through college is the "last hurdle" for many prospective retirees. If you have children, then even if college isn't exactly your "last" hurdle to retirement, it is surely one of the most significant later milestones you will pass.

Most of us in range to retire, with kids of college age, have already learned how to live prudently, control expenses, and manage investments wisely. But college tuitions can be so astronomical, and the college process is so inscrutable, that many are unwilling to pull the plug on a steady job until the kids have graduated, or at least are in sight of it. That was the case for me, and for many readers I hear from.

In my case, I *did* leave my corporate job when my son was halfway through college, because he had a scholarship that covered the majority of his expenses and I could see that he was on track to finish as planned. The few other cases I've known where people confidently retired with pre-college-aged kids were those at the upper end of the income spectrum, who had socked away 6-digit sums, in addition to their retirement nest egg, to cover their children's education.

How to assess and control college costs? The starkest divide in college tuition is between public and private schools. According to a recent version of the College Board's *Trends in College Pricing*, private schools were more than *three times* as expensive as public schools, on average. In most areas of life, you'd demand significant value before paying triple, so don't go numb on the college decision! Of course private schools do their best to distinguish their brand, and convince you they're worth the cost. But my real-life experience says that, for most majors, the school you go to for an undergraduate degree is of little consequence once you leave college behind.

Bottom line: ignore the herd instinct and find the best value in a college education for your child's particular needs. Usually, the default choice will be a public college or university in your own state.

Any *borrowing* for college should involve the same sort of hard-nosed financial analysis as starting a business. College is routinely called an "investment," but rarely analyzed like one. Will the return on the investment be greater than the costs? Can the recipient of the loan keep up with the payments? A hard look at the numbers justifies significant borrowing in only a few cases: Certain degrees or fields – medicine and engineering, for example – have a reasonable potential for retiring substantial debt. Many fields, unfortunately, do not.

Mortgage
Chances are, if you haven't paid off your house, you won't be in range to retire, because you haven't been working long enough to accumulate the required savings. True, there

are some savvy early retirees who have saved aggressively and chosen to keep carrying a low-interest-rate mortgage, but those are rare cases.

Given the definition of financial independence, anybody who holds a mortgage into retirement is doing so for cash management, not because they couldn't afford to pay it off. Perhaps their nest egg is locked away in investments that they can't easily exit without paying large capital gains taxes, or perhaps they are transitioning between homes, for example.

But the majority of retirees, myself included, will not want the complexity or uncertainty of carrying debt to be paid off in retirement, even if they can afford the payments, on paper. So, in general, for the rest of the book, we'll be assuming that your house is paid off. If not, you'll need to add in mortgage payments whenever expenses are discussed.

Consumer Debt

To retire with significant consumer debt is rarer still – simply because it is unlikely that anybody who hasn't paid off their autos or credit-card debt, for example, would have accumulated the assets needed for financial independence.

There might be some potential retirees carrying a car loan, but I encourage you to pay off loans, close out accounts, and simplify your financial life as much as possible for the discussions, and the years, ahead.

A key message of this book is that, facing the retirement decision, you're preparing for a long voyage, without a definite arrival time. There will be lots of great adventures ahead, and a few rough spots. You don't need financial distractions, such as outstanding debt – or the additional transactions and bills that represents – as you navigate your way through retirement's other challenges.

How Much Will It Cost You to Live in Retirement?

The starting point, the most critical factor and yet the most neglected one, when planning for retirement, is your *regular living expenses*. Without a deep understanding of what it costs you to live, any discussion of retirement savings or income is pointless.

Despite the oft-repeated advice that you will spend some standard percent (perhaps 60% on the low end to 100% or more on the high end) of your pre-retirement income in retirement, what it costs you to live is generally not a function of how much you make! There are millionaires who live like college students, and minimum-wage workers who live like millionaires – for a while – on credit. You're probably somewhere in between. But do you really know?

To get serious about retirement planning, you simply must have an accurate picture of the range of your monthly living expenses. You should understand what your bare *minimum* or fixed expenses need to be, what your *average* expenses should be, and what your *ideal* expenses – allowing for luxuries – could be.

Determining expenses, because it requires discipline and detail, is hard for many people. That's why it's the most neglected aspect of retirement planning. In short, the only truly accurate way to do it, is to actually *keep track of all your expenses* for at least a year, while you are living a retirement-like lifestyle, *before* actually retiring. This is one of the most important actions you can take to build wealth and retire comfortably!

You can track expenses with a desktop tool such as Quicken or an online tool such as Mint.com. But it's still time-consuming, and requires more discipline and attention to detail than many can muster. Below I'll offer some baseline numbers that you can adjust up or down for your situation. But you'll need more accuracy to be confident. How do you get that if you aren't the detail-oriented type? One approach is to sit down with a good, generic set of budget categories, plus your checking and credit card statements, and try to estimate a monthly or annual amount for each category. Don't forget those less-frequent expenses such as home and auto repairs, vacations, and property taxes!

Baselines

I'll discuss here the living expenses of couples in their 50's, no children at home, living in moderately expensive regions of the country. This is what I would call a "restrained upper-middle-class lifestyle." Think smaller houses in upscale neighborhoods, gas-efficient vehicles, few big toys or fancy clothes, careful diets, but plenty of frugal fun – road trips, coffee bars, dining out, books, and movies. In my personal experience, the minimum monthly expenses sans mortgage (assuming your house is paid for) come in at about $4,500/month, or approximately $54,000/year.

As confirmation, a reader survey at *CanIRetireYet.com* asked: "Assuming your home is paid for, about how much do you think you would need to live in retirement?" With many hundreds of responses compiled, the median answer to that question was "$4,000-$5,000/month."

And, according to bundle.com – a now-defunct web site that used aggregated spending transactions to find out how people handle their money – the average expenses (again not including mortgage or rent) for higher-income ($125K+) couples age 50-65, no kids, were about $4,675/month.

So, let's say that $4,500/month, or $54,000/year is a baseline cost of living for prospective retirees reading this book – the amount of income they must generate annually to live comfortably. (And remember, this assumes you are living in a paid-off house. Otherwise, you'll need to *add* rent to that cost of living.)

If your lifestyle sounds different, you can scale up or down as needed. For example, if you're willing to live in more modest surroundings, buy used, and eat lower on the food chain, you can probably live on quite a bit less. On the other hand, if manicured retirement communities, expensive vehicles, and international travel are your idea of retirement living, you could need quite a bit more.

Our Retirement Expenses
How will your living expenses break down in retirement? The best answer will come from tracking your own actual expenses as described above. To get you started, I'm going to review *our* major retirement expenses by budget category.

Maybe our lifestyle is similar to yours, maybe not. But it can be helpful to hear how others live and then compare their experience with yours. Take this view into our financial life for what it's worth: an example, but not a prescription. The details of our finances aren't the important point here. Use these numbers, and the following discussion, as reference points to assess and challenge *your own* living expenses.

These are our long-term averages or target for each spending category. In any given month or year, we might stray from these averages, plus or minus, by a healthy margin. We could spend more because we've had an emergency or a splurge, or we could spend less because we found some bargains or decided to save for later.

Our current retirement budget, excluding housing, is, in fact, around $4,500/month. (I'll deal more with housing costs separately, below.)

Let's break this down.…

Major Budget Categories
Groceries — We spend approximately $900/month at the grocery store. This figure also includes a number of non-grocery items such as household and personal supplies, so perhaps 75% of that number is "food." Some couples feed themselves on far less. But diet is an area that we prioritize. We buy fresh produce and organic when recommended and not exorbitantly expensive. Altogether, we think that purchasing good food is money well spent – supporting our health and a high quality of life.

Health Care — We spend about $700/month for our group health insurance plan, a retiree benefit from our former state's public school teacher retirement system. In addition to that, we budget about $500/month for medical and related health expenses: copays, deductibles, prescriptions, massages, etc. For many years we spent less than that. Recently we've been spending more. We are getting older, sigh.

Recreation — Even though it is "optional" in one sense, this is important to us, and one of our largest expenses at about $1000/month. It relates directly to the quality of our life in retirement. That figure is split about evenly between dining out, travel, and other. Those "other" expenses include outdoor gear, books, movies, shows, and classes. In a pinch, we could reduce our recreation expenses to virtually zero, by eating at home, restricting travel, and focusing on free entertainment.

Transportation — Our routine auto expenses have dropped substantially thanks to our new urban location in retirement. We currently budget about $200/month for gas, and most of that is spent during travels. We also budget about $200/month for auto repairs and maintenance. And we pay about $100/month in auto insurance. So total transportation-related expenses come to about $500/month.

Home/Office/Phone/Internet — We spend about $400/month on home upkeep and communications. We don't put money into decorating our place the way some do. Still we need furnishings occasionally, and we have minor maintenance and yard expenses, even though we are renting. We throw some money at Verizon and Comcast (the only high-speed Internet in our area) each month. We know it can be done cheaper. But these services are vital to our mobility, my blogging business, and our quality of life.

So far, we haven't had the incentive to experiment with cheaper alternatives.

Personal/Contributions/Gifts — Miscellaneous personal care expenses such as clothing, hair, etc., plus contributions and gifts, come to about $300/month. This can vary depending on the season.

Miscellaneous — Every month about $100 leaves our pockets in miscellaneous, unidentified expenses. These are cash items like snacks, parking, or tips. We've managed to reduce this amount over time, so it is of little concern now. All our major expenses are tracked using credit cards or checks. We know where our money is going with more than enough precision.

Taxes — Our modest retirement lifestyle incurs minimal income taxes – an effective state and federal tax rate in the mid-single digits, usually. Furthermore, only a portion of our living expenses must be covered by taxable income – because we have substantial after-tax accounts we can draw on. Also, since we rent, we don't pay property tax. Altogether, taxes just aren't a major expense category for us. I keep an eye on them, but if they become a consideration, it will be because our income is better than expected, and we are doing well.

Housing

I tend to write about monthly retirement living expenses separate from housing expenses. That's because the majority of people, as they approach retirement, own their homes. We did. It's not that housing is free, but it is somewhat of a sunk cost at that point, so your focus will probably be more on the other expenses discussed above.

Of course, as I explored in-depth in my article on renting vs. buying, even if you own your home, you'll be faced with plenty of ongoing house-related living expenses: insurance, maintenance, and taxes for example.

We no longer own our home, having sold it before moving to our ideal retirement relocation. So we currently pay about $1,600/month to rent a nice two-bedroom townhome in a great location. Utilities (electric, gas, water) are included, eliminating that variable from our monthly expenses.

I don't know if or when we'll buy another house. I'm in no rush. It would only happen if it made financial sense to us, was necessary to get the location we wanted, and we expected to stay put for a decade. So far that hasn't been the case at all.

Expenses Decline with Age
You can spend less in retirement than you did while you were working, and still be happy. In fact, you probably will spend less as retirement progresses, because most people don't need as much as they age.

Early in retirement you're more likely to be relocating, traveling, and spending on luxuries you missed when you were too busy working to enjoy them. Later in retirement you are more likely to be settled in your lifestyle. And, later still, with changing health and energy levels, you are even less likely to be consuming. As people reach their 70's and 80's, they aren't typically redecorating their homes or traveling the world. Their lives naturally became simpler and less active.

Government figures back this up. The Q2 2013 Consumer Expenditure Survey from the Bureau of Labor Statistics found average annual expenditures peaking at about $61,000 for the 45-54 age range. Then, expenditures fell off steadily with age. Average annual expenditures for those 55-64 were about $56,000; at 65-74 they were about $46,000; and at 75 years and older only about $34,000.

A 2012 study from the Employee Benefit Research Institute (EBRI) found a similar pattern. Household expenses declined steadily with age. Using age 65 expenses as a benchmark, household expenditures fell by 19% at age 75, 34% at age 85, and 52% at age 95.

What does this mean for the average retirement plan, which generally assumes *constant* annual expenses? Well, that's probably not realistic. If you've planned on a constant level of expenses, but spending generally tapers off as you age, then you'll probably wind up with more money than you expected in retirement.

Am I suggesting that you bank on this data and make the retirement leap even sooner, or with less assets than generally recommended? *No.* There are some technical arguments for why the news might not be quite that good. And then there is a significant caveat regarding *health care* – the one spending component that generally does *not* decline with age. The EBRI study showed that, while health care expenses are around 10% of the budget for those aged 50–64, they increase to about 20% of the budget for those age 85 and older. If health care inflation were to greatly exceed inflation in your other expense categories, or you were to have serious health or long-term care needs not covered by insurance, your overall expenses could certainly *increase* as you age.

Research shows that, for most of us, total living expenses will decrease as retirement progresses. But, it's wise to look at this general trend as "insurance" or a "bonus" if it materializes in your life, rather than making it a required element of your retirement plan.

Get Retirement Health Care

Health care is the single biggest obstacle to retirement for many. I know from surveying readers at *CanIRetireYet.com* that the cost of health care is the most common concern – trumping even running out of money, Social Security, the stock market, inflation, and taxes!

Aside from government employees, and those at a few large corporations, many of us will have serious concerns about health care coverage in our retirement years. And, given federal, state, and local budget troubles, as well as continuing economic pressures on business, even those who think they have retiree health benefits locked up may not be free from worry. Only one thing seems certain about U.S. health care: *It will cost more than we like, or be less available than we like, or both.*

I don't have all the answers, but I can offer an abbreviated guide to the current state of affairs. What follows is an overview of the entire retiree health picture: current challenges, early retirement health care options, the Patient Protection and Affordable Care Act (Obamacare), traditional retirement health care options including Medicare, and possible trends for the future. Along the way, I'll offer what I can in the way of tips for getting affordable coverage.

The Problem

The U.S. health care system, despite its technical prowess, has been in financial crisis for years. Having personally seen $20,000 in billing from a family member's routine one-day outpatient surgery, this is no surprise to me! You probably have your own stories....

Business Insider reports that health insurance premiums rose three times as fast as wages in the first decade of this century. A study published in the American Journal of Medicine indicates that 60% of personal bankruptcies are related to medical bills. Shockingly, three-fourths of the cases had health insurance, but were *still* inadequately protected.

Until the 2008 financial meltdown, health care costs had outpaced overall inflation for three decades. At times, health care inflation averaged nearly 10% – compared to a long-term average inflation rate in the neighborhood of 3%. According to the Kaiser Family Foundation, health care spending has grown by 9.6% annually since 1970 – much faster than the rate of inflation, and even 2.4% faster than the nation's Gross Domestic Product (GDP).

The math behind higher health care inflation rates is frightening. If health care starts out at 10% of your budget, but it inflates at twice the historical rate of inflation experienced by the rest of your expenses, then at the end of a 30-year retirement, health care is costing you over **20%** of your budget. And should health care inflate at *three times* the rate of your other expenses, which has been the case in the recent past, then it will consume nearly **40%** of your budget at the end of a 30-year retirement! And that is assuming you have unlimited funds to pay such expenses. The majority of us simply wouldn't have the means to keep up with that punishing rise in prices. We would forgo health care, go bankrupt, or both.

Recent news is more encouraging. But it's still early to assess the long-term trend. One reason for the recent lid on health care inflation is that health insurance has become less generous, putting more burden on patients to economize. Another is that the government has instituted cost savings in Medicare. In some cases, insurance companies and health care providers are shifting costs to other patient pools. So it's not perfectly clear yet whether health care costs are plateauing, or just changing.

More and more, government programs have become the health plans of last resort. The percentage of people who are covered by private health insurance has been decreasing steadily since 2001. As for retirees, Kaiser also reports that, continuing a long-term downward trend, only 26% of large firms offer retiree health benefits, and only 6% of small firms do.

Medicare is the U.S. public health plan for those 65 and older. It's a patchwork quilt of coverages, and has serious financial problems. We'll discuss it shortly. But let's first talk about what happens if you retire *early*....

Health Care for Early Retirees
Brace yourself for the situation you'll face if you leave your job, by choice or otherwise, before age 65. For many years there was a health insurance "gap" after employer-sponsored plans ran out, and before Medicare started at age 65.

Your possible solutions were spanned by a crazy quilt of government acronyms: COBRA, an expensive, short-term solution, and HIPAA, an expensive, long-term solution, with limited availability. If you exhausted your COBRA coverage and couldn't find or afford a HIPAA plan, then you were in the market for an *individual* health insurance plan. For those, according to one source, roughly 30-40% of people were turned down. For example, the pre-existing conditions in our generally healthy family pretty much precluded *us* from being approved for an individual plan.

Now there is a new law with benefits for early retirees and others who have difficulty getting coverage through an employer. It works, for some. But it's under both political and financial attack, and its future remains uncertain....

The Patient Protection and Affordable Care Act
The Patient Protection and Affordable Care Act (ACA), passed in 2009, often referred to as *Obamacare*, offers some hope for access to affordable health insurance for retirees. The law was fully implemented in 2014, but the rules and rates are still undergoing change.

Along with lower earners and those with pre-existing conditions, early retirees have been one of the groups most likely to benefit from the law. Key provisions include:

- a unified health insurance option available through state-based marketplaces
- a requirement that all individuals have health insurance or face a tax penalty
- a ban on insurers denying coverage or raising premiums due to pre-existing conditions
- a ban on insurers dropping policyholders who become sick

- elimination of the Medicare Part D coverage gap

How much might a basic health care plan cost an early retiree? The law envisions a "Bronze" plan with catastrophic coverage and a minimum set of essential benefits. The Congressional Budget Office estimated that premiums for Bronze plans would probably average about $395/month for single policies and about $1,020/month for family policies. However, those with income up to four times the poverty level ($64,080 for a couple in 2016) are eligible for subsidies. In the upper eligible income ranges, the subsidy would cap premiums at 9.5% of income, or a little over $500 monthly for a hypothetical couple.

Shopping Obamacare
As a potential and now actual early retiree, I've followed the new health care law closely since before its inception.

My state currently delegates its ACA exchange to the federal site: HealthCare.gov. The first thing you encounter when you access that site and look at plans is that they are categorized into five different levels: Catastrophic, Bronze, Silver, Gold, and Platinum. The government tells us that these categories are based on "how you and the plan share the costs of your care" and that the categories are not related to "the amount or quality of care you get." Supposedly, regardless of the plan you choose, you will receive the same set of pre-defined Essential Health Benefits.

But, to say that the different plans have nothing to do with the amount or quality of care you get might be misleading. The very important footnote to that statement would be "assuming you can afford to pay for what the plan does not." So, if lower-earners buy a Bronze plan because the premiums are more affordable, but then they can't afford to pay their share of health care expenses, will they really get the same care over the long run?

In terms of cost sharing, the Bronze, Silver, Gold, and Platinum plans have *actuarial values* of 60%, 70%, 80%, and 90%, respectively. (Catastrophic plans are expected to have an actuarial value of less than 60%.) "Actuarial value" means the expected out-of-pocket cost to plan participants, on average, factoring in copayments, coinsurance, and deductibles. The concept seems easy enough to understand. But when you start digging deeper, you find that it's more complex than it first appears....

For example, given the definition, I would think that plans with the same actuarial value would have the same out-of-pocket costs. And yet, according to a report from the American Academy of Actuaries, plans in a given metal tier can have *different* out-of-pocket costs, despite having the same actuarial value: "...individuals could pay more out of pocket under certain plans in a given metal tier compared to others."

And, after getting personal quotes on specific plans from HealthCare.gov, I can confirm this. Plans in the same tier *do* vary in their out-of-pocket costs. Also, there is not a clear pattern to the out-of-pocket-maximums quoted for plans in *different* tiers. Based on the government's explanation of the metal categories above, you would think that Bronze plans would always have higher out-of-pocket costs than Gold plans. Not necessarily so, it seems.

To get more information, I called eHealthInsurance.com, whose insurance agents have been helpful to me in the past. Though their plans aren't always identical to those offered through the health care exchanges, they were able to offer some clarification. They said you don't typically see variations in out-of-pocket costs between Bronze and Silver plans, at least. Rather, the difference comes in whether copays and prescriptions, for example, are counted toward the deductible or not.

Bottom line: The published out-of-pocket numbers for the various plans apparently don't reflect your true "all-in" costs. You've got quite a bit of fine print to read, and numbers to crunch, if you want to do a completely accurate comparison!

Cost-Sharing Reduction Subsidy for Silver Plans
Just when you think you have your head around the new "metallic" plan tiers, you learn that the government has created another flavor of plan:

Silver plans are "special." If you buy a Silver plan and your income is within a certain prescribed range (up to 250% of the federal poverty level), you'll receive a "cost-sharing reduction subsidy." This is money intended to reduce the cost of the actual health care *services* you receive – copayments, coinsurance, and deductibles – as opposed to reducing health insurance *premiums* (which are already reduced if your income falls under 400% of the federal poverty level). The subsidy is applied automatically and effectively shifts more of the cost onto your insurance company.

Thus, if your income is lower, you might be able to choose a Silver plan, with its lower premiums, and yet get benefits similar to a Gold or even a Platinum plan. Specifically, depending on your income level, your subsidized Silver plan could cover about 73%, 87%, or 94% of your health care costs.

Defining "Income" and MAGI

Quantifying income is fundamental to the infrastructure of the new health care law.

But there are many possible measures of income. Digging deeper, what does the government mean by "income" in the context of the new law? By and large it means, not Taxable Income, and not Adjusted Gross Income, but something called *Modified Adjusted Gross Income* or MAGI.

In many cases, MAGI will simply be your Adjusted Gross Income, found at the bottom of the first page of your Form 1040. Just beware that both of these numbers, which are critical to computing your health care benefits, are usually substantially larger than your Taxable Income. And note that AGI and MAGI include your *capital gains*, even though, by virtue of your tax bracket, you may not be taxed on them. Also, MAGI includes any tax-exempt interest income.

The new law is designed for people whose income level doesn't change much from year to year. It assumes you have constant income within some narrow range. But, for early retirees living off investment assets, who experience both some unpredictability and some degree of control over when they realize income, the costs and benefits of the new law are not immediately obvious.

Do you sequence your withdrawals so you can qualify for specific Premium Credits and the Cost-Sharing Reduction Subsidy in certain years? What happens in other years when you have larger gains or distributions? Will your health care costs fluctuate widely with your realized income? While the new health care law has provided some assurances as to coverage and costs, it has left plenty of remaining implementation questions, at least for early retirees.

Comparing Plans

HealthCare.gov now offers an option to browse available plans and estimate your annual costs, without logging in or completing an application. This is accessed under Get Coverage - See Plans & Prices. You enter basic data, and then get a preview of your potential choices. If you're eligible for a tax credit to lower your monthly premium costs, you will see that reflected in premiums for the plans displayed.

The government's site offers some capabilities for comparison shopping: You can narrow results using filters for premium, categories, types, companies, and programs. You can manually compare plan parameters such as premium, deductible, out-of-pocket maximum, copayments, and coinsurance.

There were a total of 52 health plans available to us in our state. Bronze plans featured premiums of $105-$478/month. Silver plans were $258-$624/month. Gold plans were $385-

$849/month. The single available Platinum plan was $884/month.

For comparison purposes I ran a similar query at eHealthInsurance.com, then called and spoke with one of their agents. In federal exchange states like ours, plus a few others, you can supposedly buy the identical government-subsidized plans that are available from the federal Marketplace – though they didn't appear identical to me on quick inspection. They also offer "private" plans, without a subsidy.

My Analysis

I analyzed the coverage offered by available plans using my own spreadsheet. In essence, I collected the premium, deductible, coinsurance percent, and out-of-pocket maximum for a subset of plans that seemed attractive to us. (Generally the larger insurance companies with more extensive provider networks.) I assumed we would receive a premium tax credit based on our projected income. Then I calculated what our actual, all-in health care costs (including premiums) would be for years in which we experienced one of six possible medical scenarios: $0, $1,000, $5,000, $10,000, $20,000, and $50,000 in medical expenses.

The end results constitute the most complete picture I've gotten of how health insurance works generally, and how it applies to us, personally:

The bottom line is that there is less economic difference between plans than you might expect, especially if you experience significant medical expenses. The ACA prescribes out-of-pocket maximum limits for all plans sold through the Marketplace. In 2016 that limit is $13,700 for a family plan. So, by the time you reach very high-expense medical scenarios in the $40,000-$50,000 range, most of the plans hit their out-of-pocket maximums and cost roughly the same overall. The difference between the cheapest and most expensive PPO plan was only about 18%. That's a few thousand dollars in a bad year for medical expenses – probably not a deal breaker.

If you don't experience high-expense medical scenarios, then the differences between plans are relatively larger, more a function of the premium than the out-of-pocket maximum. Which plan is more financially advantageous for you comes down to your exact medical expenses. If those expenses are low, then the Bronze plans – with lower premiums and higher deductibles – may offer the best value. If your expenses are higher, then the Silver or Gold plans, with relatively higher premiums and relatively lower deductibles, could be more optimal.

Retiree Health Benefits and the New Law
How does the new law apply to those who have pre-Medicare retiree health benefits? For starters, as might be expected, if you've got retiree health benefits, then the new law *does* consider you to be insured – meaning you don't have to worry about paying penalties for *not* having health insurance.

But, the big question is this: "Should you give up existing retirement health insurance benefits in hopes of purchasing less expensive insurance through the exchanges?"

Your answer will be complex and personal. I've already presented some of the numbers required for a financial analysis. You'll want to update those with the latest data from HealthCare.gov. Beyond that, I can only offer my conclusion for our personal situation: Given roughly comparable costs, and the political and financial uncertainty around Obamacare, we won't be switching.

If you *do* decide to drop your retirement health benefits in favor of Obamacare, be extremely cautious about the details and *the* timing. Consult the <u>instructions for retirees</u> on HealthCare.gov carefully and beware this provision:

*"If you voluntarily drop your retiree coverage, you **won't** qualify for a Special Enrollment Period to enroll in a new Marketplace plan. You won't be able to enroll in health coverage through the Marketplace until the next Open Enrollment period."*

Optimizing Obamacare

The ACA has transformed the landscape for early retirees with pre-existing conditions in the U.S. We can now get health insurance at reasonable rates, at least in some areas. (The cost varies by location and can still be very expensive.)

But, for those who want to understand and optimize their health care finances, the new law creates new problems: Superimposing the ACA and federal income tax profiles makes for a bewildering puzzle at tax time. Even the financially savvy will be hard-pressed to minimize all their costs, especially if life events don't cooperate.

The problem is the number of constraints that come into play: You can't make too *much* income, or you'll lose subsidies. You also can't make too *little* income, or you'll be forced onto Medicaid or lose coverage.

The way the Premium Tax Credit is reduced as income increases, works like a tax. At incomes above 400% of the Federal Poverty Level (FPL), subsidies are completely eliminated. This is known as the "Premium Subsidy Cliff." It's a *cliff* because, in high-cost areas, $1 of additional income could expose you to thousands of dollars in increased premium expenses!

Roth conversions and tax-free capital gains harvesting are other key tax strategies whose thresholds are complicated by the new ACA rules.

Given the current system, which subsidizes health care via the tax code, if you are retired and relying on Obamacare, and want to minimize your expenses, you will have no choice but to become an expert on taxes.

Most early retirees and even many traditional retirees have some flexibility in how they realize income. You can control the timing for when you claim Social Security, withdraw from retirement accounts, harvest capital gains, take on part-time work, and pay certain major expenses. Each of these events impacts your income, and thus your eligibility for ACA subsidies.

Here is the general strategy for optimizing insurance savings through the ACA exchanges in early retirement:

1. Start by tracking your income carefully during the year: It's the most vital metric for using the ACA.

2. Be sure to generate enough income to exceed 138% of the Federal Poverty Level in states that expanded Medicaid, or 100% of the FPL in states that did not.

3. Maximize benefits by keeping your MAGI between 100%-250% of FPL and choosing a Silver plan, to be eligible for the Cost Sharing Subsidy Reduction. That gives you lower out-of-pocket costs on copayments, coinsurance, and/or deductibles.

4. Do whatever you can to stay below 400% of the FPL, to avoid losing subsidies altogether and possibly going over the premium "cliff." (Strategies include making IRA, spousal IRA, or HSA contributions before tax returns are due the following year.)

Other Health Care Options for Early Retirees
If government programs don't fit you financially, or philosophically, there are a few alternatives to Obamacare that bypass the traditional health insurance model:

The first is Direct Primary Care (DPC), which replaces the typical fee-for-service insurance model with a simple flat monthly fee that covers routine primary care services. This makes your expenses, at least for routine health care, more predictable. Examples of DPC include Qliance in Washington state, and MedLion, now expanding across the country. In some cases, DPC can be coupled with Health Savings Accounts (HSAs), or high-deductible health insurance, to cover major medical care, though the rules are still being established.

Related to DPC are higher-end "concierge medicine" practices where a group of patients pay an annual retainer and receive exclusive access to their doctor. According to knowledgeable insiders, such practices may thrive in a few well-to-do locations, but will have difficulty keeping up with the infrastructure demands of modern medicine, particularly in information technology systems.

Finally, there are the faith-based health care ministries, which function like private insurance pools for groups willing to live by similar beliefs. Members pool their resources when they're healthy, to provide for times when they're not. In these plans, everybody pays equally and is eligible for equal benefits. No government regulations or insurance company rules are involved. But payments aren't guaranteed either. They depend on cash flow. In general, the plans seem to work: You'll find many reports online of high satisfaction and significantly lower premiums and deductibles than Obamacare.

Currently there are *five* such ministries with critical mass: Liberty HealthShare, Medi-Share, Christian Healthcare Ministries, Samaritan Ministries, and Altrua HealthShare.

Health Savings Accounts linked to high-deductible health insurance policies have been used for years by the healthy or self-employed to control health care premiums. But you must have the resources to cover out-of-pocket expenses up to your deductible. If you wind up paying the full deductible every year, the plan could prove to be very expensive.

If you are willing to work part-time in retirement, there are some prominent companies that offer health benefits for part-time workers. Here are some of the more recognizable and accessible names that have offered such benefits at one time or another: Costco, Home Depot, JC Penney, Land's End, Lowes, Nordstrom, REI, The Container Store, Staples, Starbucks, Target, Trader Joe's, and Whole Foods.

Health Care for Traditional Retirees: Original Medicare

Medicare, created in 1965, is the public health plan in the U.S. for people 65 or older. It's available to all, regardless of health history. The uninitiated may view Medicare as monolithic "free public health," but in fact, it's a patchwork quilt of free and paid elements....

Medicare is divided into *four* parts. Part A covers hospital and other health facility care. Part B covers doctors' services and outpatient care. Those who paid Medicare taxes during their working career get Medicare Part A for "free" but still must pay a deductible ($1,288 in 2016) plus copays and percentages for various charges.

Medicare Part B requires paying a premium, about $105 monthly in 2016 (which is usually automatically deducted from your Social Security payments), and a deductible ($166 in 2016), plus a percentage of various services.

Medicare Add-Ons

Medicare Part C, known as "Medicare Advantage," is run by private insurance companies, and generally *includes*

Parts A, B, and D (prescription drug coverage) *plus* other health care options such as vision or dental. Each plan's cost structure is different, but generally, they resemble conventional health insurance with deductibles, copayments, and managed care from doctors/hospitals in a certain network. The Medicare Part C plans generally incorporate the Part B premium, plus other charges, to cover their additional options.

Medicare Part D, also run by private insurance companies, helps cover prescription drug costs. To get Part D, you must join a private insurance plan, either a Part C plan or a dedicated Prescription Drug Plan. These plans generally charge a monthly fee, a yearly deductible (capped at $360 in 2016), and copayments/coinsurance for each of your prescriptions.

Finally, you can also purchase supplementary "Medigap" plans that add to original Medicare by covering copayments, coinsurance, and deductibles to some extent. These plans come in standardized versions. The costs vary by policy, company, and area. In general, if you have a Medicare Advantage Plan, you don't get a Medigap plan.

The Future of Medicare
In describing Medicare with a few paragraphs, I've intentionally simplified what is a very complex government program. You'll need to visit Medicare.gov for many important details. And, if you are nearing age 65, pay special attention to the various prescribed enrollment periods, because there are penalties for not enrolling at those specific times!

Unfortunately, due to an aging population and soaring health care costs, Medicare is the most financially unstable of the major government social programs. Though projections are highly uncertain, here are a couple of statistical nuggets from a recent report from the Medicare Trustees: (1) Medicare's costs are expected to nearly *double* as a percent of GDP within the next 30 years; (2) the trust fund underlying Part A is expected to be *out of money* in little more than a decade.

As an essential social safety net, Medicare is unlikely to go away, but its scope is uncertain. As a new or prospective retiree, what you need to know is this: Benefits certainly won't increase, and are highly likely to *decrease* over the course of your retirement. Unfortunately, the more you anticipate major medical expenses and the more you rely solely on Medicare – without supplemental insurance – the more financial risk you will be taking on in retirement.

The Future of Obamacare
The future of Obamacare is equally uncertain. The Right wants to gut it, the Left wants to tweak or expand it. Given such a new and volatile program, any election year could bring dramatic change.

And, even without political changes, there are worrisome indicators for financial stability: Actuaries question whether Obamacare will be financially sustainable if current usage trends continue.

Major insurers have abandoned unprofitable Obamacare business in some markets and more are threatening to leave.

There are reports of sick people gaming the system, while healthy people avoid it. Some experts advise using the ACA exchanges only if you're getting a subsidy: That might be a good personal strategy, but it's not financially sustainable for a country. (Insurance doesn't work if only the people in need buy it.) If these trends continue, Obamacare could be bankrupt in a few years.

If Obamacare fails, will the U.S. health care system take some other route to expanded coverage? The interests vested in the current system are numerous, wealthy, and powerful. Expecting significant change any time soon looks like wishful thinking to me.

However, one aspect of the ACA that we can probably count on continuing is the ban on denying coverage, dropping coverage, or raising premiums due to your medical condition. Those provisions will be too politically popular to get axed.

While not the roadblock it once was, health insurance remains both uncertain and expensive for U.S. retirees. And no resolution is in sight. Naturally, you'll try to optimize your health care spending. But, given the pressures and changes afoot, no single strategy is likely to carry you all the way through retirement. Staying informed and flexible, *and healthy*, is your best hope.

How I Got Retirement Health Insurance
The most reliable strategy for retirement health care is one that starts relatively early in your career, and, unfortunately, won't suit everyone. *Public service* – working for a government entity – is the only path that seems to offer

some certainty of retiree health benefits going forward. I don't see the elimination of health care for our veterans or retired public safety workers any time soon, though benefits could certainly be reduced.

However, in the private sector, even the most compassionate and profitable corporations are under relentless pressure to cut back on health care benefits, and they certainly won't be looking for reasons to extend those benefits to employees after they've left the work force.

As for my personal experience? My previous employer, a progressive and well-managed midsize company with generous employee benefits, had nothing to offer retiring employees with decades of service. When I retired, after enjoying a premium health plan for decades, we were looking at an abyss until age 65.

So, how, in the face of all the problems outlined above, was I able to leave my career at age 50?

Well, I married the right woman years ago. Among many other wonderful attributes, she was a public school teacher and qualified for group retiree health benefits that also cover dependents. So, after I retired, and we had been on COBRA for a few months, we switched our family coverage to *her* health plan.

The benefits could be threatened by ongoing local budget crises. But, for now, they are our best bet. We also have to pay for them. It's a group plan so the costs are controlled, but they are anything but cheap. When I retired five years ago, I budgeted what I thought would be generously for our health care. I knew these costs could be the single biggest risk factor in our retirement. So I planned on $700/month for health insurance premiums. And I also budgeted $500/month for out-of-pocket health care expenses.

How is it going? We are fast approaching that premium figure. The next inflation adjustment to our health insurance premium will likely put us over. As for out-of-pocket expenses, more months than not, we are spending our full budgeted amount. Together those two categories make $1200/month or over $14K year in health care expenses. So, already, in our mid-50's, we are close to exceeding our health care budget. It's a worrisome trend for our future.

Keep an Eye on Inflation

We've discussed the issues and options for retirement health care, which is likely to be one of your largest and most unpredictable retirement expenses. What about the growth in your other expenses? How much of a toll should you expect inflation to take on your spending power over the course of retirement?

In my first book, *Retiring Sooner*, I discussed your personal rate of inflation and how, based on my experience, and that of other real-world retirees, it's probably much less than the official government rate. I showed how a combination of advancing technology and old-fashioned frugality could tame at least some of inflation's bite. A key takeaway is that you should monitor and react to *your own* rate of inflation, not the official figures.

However, I pointed to some areas, such as housing and health care, where inflation might be out of our immediate control. In sum, inflation *could be* a real threat to your retirement. But, if it continues as it has the last decade or two, it's probably not the threat it is often made out to be. Unfortunately, that is a significant "*if.*"

Loose monetary policy from the Federal Reserve in recent years has been unprecedented. Today's razor-thin interest rates and low yields are historic extremes, and they are coupled with the government's inability to spend within its means. So many experts predict that higher inflation is inevitable in our future. That possibility is one you'd be wise to incorporate when planning for retirement. Especially over long time spans, inflation can damage your investment returns and reduce your spending power to a fraction of what it once was.

But a puzzle remains: Despite a decade of warnings from monetary hawks, extreme inflation hasn't appeared yet, and frankly doesn't seem to be on the immediate horizon. The average rate of inflation (CPI-U) in the U.S. for the 21st century of about 2.2% is actually well below the historical average of about 3.3%. The more common fear in recent times has been one of low inflation or even *deflation* – usually associated with economic contraction.

A reasonable conclusion would be that, while inflation remains a strong possibility in the future, it's not an immediate threat. Trouble is, retirement time frames extend well into the period when severe inflation *could* become a problem. So, will it rise precipitously as many predict? And, if so, when?

I can't predict the future. I suspect that inflation will continue to be used as a political issue, and that the reality won't be as extreme as either side predicts. Inflation will likely remain within historical norms, or perhaps a little higher. But, inflation has proven no more predictable than the stock market, so don't bank your future on knowing it.

For now, let's discuss where inflation comes from and what you can do to protect yourself if it reappears. By educating yourself, understanding inflation at a deeper level, and watching carefully for its possible reappearance, you can be better prepared to combat its potential effects. And, you can take some modest steps to prepare for it now, without costing yourself too much, regardless of how the future turns out.

A Money Tale

First I'm going to offer a high-level picture of how the money supply works, and how it interacts with our political machinery. Then I'm going to let you in on *two secrets* that you won't read about in the mainstream media, on either side of the political aisle.

Let's start by understanding that, despite its mystique, "money" is a human invention. It's nothing more than a social convention for keeping score of wealth. If you doubt this, take out a dollar bill to gaze at and ask yourself how much value it would have if you were stuck alone on a desert island, or on the moon. This is why some people refer to it as "fiat" currency. That bill has value because the government says so. If you go someplace where the government doesn't value it, it's worthless.

Though money appears to be physically created from paper and metal, in fact a primary mechanism for "creating" money is *debt*. To see how this works, suppose you lived several millennia ago, in a time before currency, and you did some carpentry work for neighbors in the village. Perhaps they paid you by writing an IOU on a piece of parchment. You knew they were skilled farmers, and you trusted they would return that value to you down the road. So, no problem.

The next day you visit your local shopkeeper to buy some flour. The shopkeeper knows your neighbors too, so in payment for the flour, you trade him that paper IOU from the day before. Now your neighbors owe the shopkeeper, not you. The shopkeeper will collect down the road as needed.

See what happened? Paper money was born, through debt. This works well enough as long as everybody writing IOU's remains personally responsible for doing the work to pay back those debts. A closed system among neighbors works pretty well. But then stresses appear. The most productive villagers accumulate lots of notes. A bad crop year sweeps through and leaves the farmers without any purchasing power....

So the kingdom creates a *central bank* to "regulate" the money supply, smoothing out the negative effects of these natural cycles. That central bank decides that everybody would be better off if the economy were "stimulated" with more and more IOU's in circulation. So it begins printing IOU's of its own.

But these IOU's are different somehow. Even though they look the same, no work was performed, no value was created, along with them. To get them into circulation quickly, the central bank gives these IOU's out for free to anybody who will fill out a credit application and promise to pay them back with interest.

Voilà, the money supply "grows," and suddenly there are more people spending more IOU's. Shopkeepers are happy with the increased sales. Everything looks good, for a while.

But something isn't quite right behind the scenes. Because the new IOU's are somehow unhinged from the issuer's ability to pay. And the effect of that unhinging in the shops is this: There are more IOU's chasing the same amount of goods.

The law of supply and demand kicks in, and prices go up. That's *inflation*.

Even worse, those people who had saved IOU's for a rainy day, or a retirement, find that they buy less now than they used to. Some of their wealth has mysteriously disappeared, even though nobody broke in and stole from them. How did it happen?

Two Secrets

Most people accept inflation as a necessary evil, inherent to modern monetary systems. But what is inflation exactly? Well, here is the **first secret**, the straight scoop, which you won't often read in the mainstream press: Inflation is essentially a mechanism to transfer wealth from one segment of society to another. It is a hidden tax on savers and their savings, imposed by governments intent on redistributing wealth for other purposes.

In making inflation versus employment tradeoffs, the Federal Reserve is weighing between the haves and have-nots. That may sound like political rhetoric, but I have no agenda here. This is just the economic reality. The recipients of this largesse and their political leaders would rather you not understand this. But inflation is essentially wealth distribution from the minority of the wealthy and savers to the majority of consumers and borrowers. That's not fair or "right" by some measures. But it is *reality*, so you should prepare to live with some degree of it in retirement.

Governments have the power to print more money (physically or electronically) at any time to spend on their own priorities. When they do, they devalue the value of the currency that you hold. Over time, inflation is no different than a tax. At the end of a year with 3% inflation, your savings has 3% less spending power. And whoever the government decides to favor with its largesse has 3% more.

Now for the **second secret**: the world's wealth is far more *concentrated* than most people imagine. According to an analysis of the Federal Reserve's Survey of Consumer Finances for 2007, the top 1% of families in the U.S. hold 35% of the wealth, and the top 10% hold nearly *three-quarters* of all the country's wealth!

Most of the wealthy and savers would rather this not be known. They may not like it, but they can probably afford a lot more inflation and wealth distribution than they let on. But they are afraid that if they give an inch, consumers and borrowers will take a mile. Which they probably will....

Most of the conflict in the world boils down to a struggle over resources: between those who own them, and those who feel they don't have enough. Where you consider yourself to be on this spectrum, and what you think the future holds for each group, dictates how you should prepare for the future.

What It Means to You

Though everybody is affected by inflation, only those with saved wealth (comfortable retirees, by definition) have much to fear. For the rest, consumers and borrowers, the benefits will outrun the costs, at least if the inflating process remains orderly.

For the retirees, who are threatened by inflation, it is wise to understand the difference between baseline or "expected" inflation and a potential spike or "unexpected" inflation. Baseline inflation of about 3% annually is built into most retirement models and economic projections. As long as you own diverse assets, including a house and a significant percentage of stocks among your investments, you have little to fear from continued baseline or expected inflation. It's like those 1% credit card kickbacks – an unnecessary overhead, but one that the system is geared for and everybody expects.

But what if the pessimists are right and current government policies lead to a sudden spike in inflation: double-digit inflation rates like the 1970's or even "hyperinflation," where the value of cash holdings can erode almost overnight through arbitrary government actions and black market activity?

On one hand, I don't believe in spending much time or money trying to prepare for any of the many extraordinary events that might occur over a decades-long retirement. By definition, whatever you're preparing for in the "black swan" category, probably will not occur in the way you imagine.

On the other hand, there are several time-tested investments that will fare reasonably well in normal times while providing a hedge against extraordinary inflation as well. If you're concerned about the potential for abnormal inflation, then you might choose to buy an "insurance policy" against the unexpected or hyperinflation scenario.

The list of inflation-fighting investments that I've held over the years include TIPS (Treasury Inflation-Protected Securities), real estate, natural resources, and gold. Though academics will debate whether these will outperform baseline inflation, there is little doubt in my mind that, as *physical* assets, all would do well against hyperinflation.

Gold, in particular, has a several-millennium-long track record as a stable asset in volatile times. The simplest, cheapest, safest way to own gold in modern times is through an exchange traded fund such as SPDR Gold Shares (GLD). For myself, a 5-10% position in gold has felt appropriate in my retirement portfolio for many years. You'll have to assess your own situation and decide what, if anything, is right for you.

Just remember that all insurance has a *cost*, which will likely come in the form of underperformance during normal times. But you don't buy insurance for normal times. Those savers who are concerned about the prospects for abnormal inflation will want at least some stake in their portfolios from the above list of proven inflation fighters.

But Don't Fret About Taxes

On either side of the aisle these days, it's not politically correct to be ambivalent about taxes. If you lean to the left, you're supposed to feel the tax code should be more progressive, that taxes should be higher on the wealthy and on corporations. And if you lean to the right, you're supposed to think there should be less taxes, less spending, less government all around.

And, many of us of any persuasion wish the tax code were *simpler*. Though, those who make their living in politics or finance might feel that the astoundingly complex U.S. tax code is fine as it is. After all, fear and confusion related to paying taxes is one of the primary drivers pushing customers or voters their way!

But I'm not in any of those camps. I don't have any special expertise or interest in taxes, and I purposefully don't write about them much. (There are many other excellent sources of tax information available: Mike Piper's *Oblivious Investor* blog is one.)

I have no interest in pushing a particular viewpoint on taxation. I'm just an early retiree in the middle of the road, who lives frugally, and wants to keep life simple. I'm interested in the *current reality* we all have to live in for retirement, whether we agree with it or not. Perhaps it comes as a surprise, but taxes are just *not* a primary concern of mine....

My philosophy is to keep my financial life simple, live frugally at low tax rates, and then pay my share, without squabbling. The complexity and conniving that our tax code seems to invite, feels like a colossal waste of time to me.

The Tax Bogeyman

There is such revulsion to taxes in the U.S. that the tendency is to overestimate their impact, especially at lower and middle income levels. The tax structure actually *doesn't* impact a frugal *early* retiree leading a modest lifestyle very much, because much of our income has already been taxed, or is taxed at lower rates. *Effective tax rates* (your total tax paid divided by gross income) are surprisingly low at income levels that will suffice for many of us to enjoy a comfortable retirement.

What about *traditional* retirees – somebody who is collecting Social Security or a pension and living off primarily traditional retirement accounts? In that case, more of your income *will* be taxable. In some cases, generally when Required Minimum Distributions start and combine with Social Security payments in your 70's, marginal tax rates can reach alarming levels. But those rates generally only kick in for restricted ranges of income, and can be reduced, if you're concerned, using well-known tax strategies such as Roth conversions.

Yet many people with agendas – from politicians to bankers to financial planners – want you to believe that taxes will make or break your financial success. One retirement site went so far as to say that the #1 goal of retirement savings and spending should be to minimize taxes. *Sorry, but I'm retired and I'm just not seeing that.*

Another respected site says that taxes are your single biggest expense. But that's not true in my experience either. We easily spend more each month on gas, groceries, health insurance, and travel than we do on taxes.

When I was a few months from pulling the plug on my career, I went for a free consultation with a local financial planner at a respected regional firm. When they ran the projections for my retirement they used a 20% *effective* tax rate! They were assuming that one in five of my retirement income dollars would disappear to taxes. As I'll shortly demonstrate, that was wildly inappropriate. Their mistake likely stemmed from taking a *marginal* tax rate (the amount paid on the last dollar of income), and applying it to *all* of our retirement income, disregarding the substantial portion which would be taxed at a much lower rate, or exempt from taxes. The end result grossly overstated our tax liability in retirement.

The Law
What is taxed in retirement? Here is a simplified overview:

Table: Income Taxation

Tax Free	Taxable
Income below the standard deduction + exemptions	Income above the standard deduction + exemptions
Qualified dividends/long-term capital gains in 10-15% bracket	Qualified dividends/long-term capital gains in 25% bracket and above
Social Security below combined income threshold	50-85% of Social Security above threshold
Roth retirement account withdrawals	Traditional retirement account withdrawals
Taxable account withdrawals	

As a reminder, the lower tax rates on those married and filing jointly as this is written (tax year 2016) are as follows:

- 10% on taxable income from $0 to $18,550
- 15% on taxable income over $18,551 to $75,300
- 25% on taxable income over $75,301 to $151,900

It's not uncommon to hear financial pundits warning that some new legislation will impact retirees and baby boomers who rely on investment income. But that's rarely the case. Washington usually spares the middle class.

In the last round of changes to taxes on capital gains and dividends, rates only increased for couples making more than $450,000/year. That level of income is not remotely representative of the typical retiree. You can enjoy a grand retirement on a fraction of that.

The Numbers: A Frugal Retiree's Tale

Now that we've covered basic tax concepts and laws, let's look at some real-life examples. The survey at *CanIRetireYet.com* mentioned earlier asked: "Assuming your home is paid for, about how much do you think you would need to live in retirement?"

The median answer to that question was "$4,000-$5,000/month." So we estimated that $4,500/month, or $54,000/year would be the average cost of living for prospective retirees reading this book, the amount of income they must generate annually to live comfortably.

I know that if you live in an expensive area, or have a more luxurious lifestyle, your number could be considerably higher than that, and some of what I say here may not apply to you. On the other hand, for the many people who require even less in retirement, what I say here is even more applicable.

For tax year 2016, the standard deduction for a married couple filing jointly is $12,600, and the personal exemption is $4,050 each. So that makes exactly $20,700 of retirement income, for a couple, which is not taxed at all.

For our average retired couple that leaves, worst case, $33,300 in taxable income needed to cover the proposed $54,000 budget. Given the tax rates listed above, the first $18,550 will be taxed at 10%, and the remainder at 15%. Run those numbers and that means paying about $4,067 in taxes annually, or about $340 a month.

That is, worst case, a 7.5% effective tax rate on the original $54,000 income. Most retirees will pay less, some much less. Why? For starters, that calculation assumed you had no additional tax deductions or credits. (In our case in recent years, for example, medical expenses have been high enough to earn us an additional itemized deduction.)

But for *early* retirees there is a more significant factor: A big chunk of our savings (about half) is in *after-tax* accounts, where only new gains or income could be taxed. (Many other retirees will have Roth accounts with similar tax characteristics.) So, as early retirees, much of the money we consume in the early years of retirement is either taxed at a lower rate, as investment income, or isn't taxed at all!

Just because you have an expense in retirement doesn't mean you're going to have to pay full income tax on a comparable amount of income. The money for paying that expense could come via withdrawals from an already-taxed account, or it could come from capital gains which are taxed at a lower rate, or not at all. In fact, qualified dividends and long-term capital gains that fall into the 10% or 15% tax bracket, *are not even taxed!*

The bottom line: I expect to be paying an effective income tax rate of less than 5% in my early retirement years. And, given the other variables in the retirement equation – investment returns, inflation, Social Security, health care – that small percent in income taxes falls well down my list of concerns....

How much can *you* expect to pay? Here are the current monthly taxes and effective federal tax rates for typical income levels in retirement. (Note this does *not* include any additional tax-reducing impacts of your personal tax deductions). Also included in the table are the taxes and effective rates if 50% of the total income is from capital gains, meaning only *half* of that income is taxable in the lower tax brackets:

Table: **Effective Tax Rates**

Monthly Income	Monthly Tax	Effective Rate	Monthly Tax (50%)	Effective Rate (50%)
$2,000	$28	1.4%	$0	0.0%
$2,500	$78	3.1%	$0	0.0%
$3,000	$128	4.3%	$0	0.0%
$3,500	$189	5.4%	$3	0.1%
$4,000	$264	6.6%	$28	0.7%
$4,500	$339	7.5%	$53	1.2%
$5,000	$414	8.3%	$78	1.6%
$5,500	$489	8.9%	$103	1.9%
$6,000	$564	9.4%	$128	2.1%
$6,500	$639	9.8%	$153	2.3%
$7,000	$714	10.2%	$189	2.7%
$7,500	$789	10.5%	$226	3.0%
$8,000	$864	10.8%	$264	3.3%
$8,500	$989	11.6%	$376	4.4%
$9,000	$1,114	12.4%	$489	5.4%

The Fate of the Middle Class

Will the middle class remain safe from tax increases? Who knows? But I'm not particularly worried. Because, even if the major middle-class tax breaks are removed, it would be unlikely to impact frugal retirees much. The largest target affecting the middle class may be employer health insurance, given that workers with employer-sponsored health coverage don't have to pay taxes on the share of premiums paid by the company. The other two prominent middle-class tax breaks are the mortgage interest deduction and tax-deferral of retirement plan contributions. And changes to any of those items would be unlikely to affect the lifestyles of those at or near retirement.

Yes, the U.S. is in debt and there are bills to be paid. There is a widespread belief that taxes will somehow go up on most of us in retirement. Yet one political party is committed to *no* taxes, while the other party is committed to raising taxes only on the wealthy. And the middle class is largely responsible for electing them both. I don't see how those realities lead to tax increases on middle-income retirees. Inflation, yes, but substantial tax increases, no.

This May Not Apply to You If...

Of course, there are some situations where this relaxed attitude towards taxes does not work. For those with bigger expenses, and bigger incomes, tax impacts might be more substantial. If you live in a high tax state, then state income taxes could add substantially to the federal tax I've been discussing. (Though you'd be wise to re-evaluate your retirement location if feasible.) Perhaps you have the good fortune to be living on a multiple-six-digit income in retirement. If so, congratulations on your success in life. And, yes, your taxes have probably gone up, and may do so again. People in these groups may be required to make some lifestyle changes, especially if they have been consuming nearly all their income each year.

Like most people, I'd be happy to pay less in taxes. But I'm not interested in arguing here whether our current tax system is fair or unfair, or whether certain segments of society should or shouldn't pay more in taxes, or whether the government does or doesn't know how to spend our money better than we do. Taxes are a low-priority issue for me, because they haven't been critical in my own retirement yet. They aren't trivial, but they also aren't going to wreck our budget, or change our lifestyle.

And, there is one final reason I don't fret about taxes: Because, aside from taking a few simple financial measures, and voting, *there is very little I can do about them!*

Take Action

- Pay off debt and create savings to cover any lingering major life expenses, especially college for kids.
- Estimate your retirement budget – your monthly living expenses – based on those with a similar lifestyle, or your own records. Live on that budget for a few years, before making the leap to retirement.
- Line up your retirement health care. If you don't have a retirement health plan from work, know how the Obamacare exchanges or Medicare apply to you.
- Understand the deeper workings of inflation, and its impact on your savings. If you're concerned about preserving your wealth in the face of higher than normal inflation, investigate and choose a modest allocation to inflation-fighting investments.
- Compute your *effective* tax rate in retirement, so you can understand the true impact of taxes on your own retirement budget.

2: UNDERSTANDING YOUR RETIREMENT INCOME

"You're never truly financially free until your passive investment income exceeds expenses (and even that has limitations due to inflation and changing business conditions). As long as you depend on asset growth for any part of spending then you are in a race against inflation, market fluctuations and time." — Todd Tresidder

Next we'll explore all your possible sources of retirement income. We'll start with the assets you've accrued from your employment history: pensions and Social Security. Then we'll talk about your nest egg, which is probably in an investment portfolio, and how it might be managed for income. We'll explore the two prevailing philosophies for generating retirement income: relying on stock market probabilities versus putting safety first with insurance. Then we'll introduce annuities and the possibility that you will need to annuitize a portion of your nest egg, in order to meet your retirement income needs. Finally, we'll explore working in retirement, out of financial or emotional necessity, or just because it's the path you choose to give back to the world. And we'll conclude with a look at the benefits of drawing on all or most of these multiple income sources as you construct your "retirement paycheck."

Pensions and Future Income

My grandfather, a railroad employee and executive, had a pension. My father, a naval officer, had a pension. I don't, and neither will most of my peers and readers. The working world has changed in the last century.

I began my career out of college working for the federal government for two years. That was my last opportunity to participate in a traditional pension plan. Despite a successful career that encompassed working for three profitable private companies ranging in size from a few dozen, to a hundred, to thousands, of employees – I never again was offered that golden opportunity.

Over the last three decades – essentially the span of my own working career – the traditional pension plan has died a slow death. The disappearance of defined-benefit pensions and the erosion of the Social Security system make modern retirements far less certain than those of the recent past.

CBS News reports that only 11% of the Fortune 1000 companies now offer a traditional pension plan to new salaried workers. That's down from 90% in 1985! This is more hard evidence, if you weren't already aware, of the major sea change in how the United States prepares for retirement. In essence that change boils down to a shift in responsibility for retirement planning and saving from *institutions* to *individuals*.

Few employees are offered a traditional pension plan at work anymore. According to the Employee Benefit Research Institute, today only about 15% of private-sector workers have a pension that guarantees a steady payout during retirement. Unless you are a union member or public servant, chances are you will not have a pension.

The guaranteed lifetime income, usually inflation-adjusted, offered by a traditional pension plan is an extremely valuable, and increasingly rare, asset in today's world. That reliable lifelong income stream would significantly enhance your retirement security, while reducing your required retirement savings.

In general, this book assumes that, like most of us, you won't have a traditional pension when you retire. Since the vast majority of baby boomer and later generations will not receive pensions, we'll only deal with them briefly here.

The primary question around a pension at retirement involves "How much is it worth?" and the related question: "Should you take it as regular payments or as a lump sum?" It's not possible to offer a universal answer. You need to crunch the numbers to see what makes sense in your case. However, if you want a *default* answer, until you are able to perform a more in-depth analysis, it would be to take the regular payments. Here's one example of why:

Because my wife worked only part-time while we were raising our son, and because she taught in different states and cashed out of various plans over her career, she was entitled to only a very small pension (on the order of $100/month) when she recently retired. However, even though this small amount makes little difference in our retirement security, and could even be a bookkeeping hassle, we took it. Why? Because, along with Social

Security, it represents our only *guaranteed, inflation-adjusted lifetime income*. And that is priceless.

To demonstrate why, I calculated the "Annual Payout Rate." That is the percentage of the lump sum we were offered which would be paid back to us each year if we elected regular payments. (For the record, those payments include both interest and return of principal, so they can be significantly higher than a conventional interest payment.) In our case, taking the regular payouts constituted more than an 8% Annual Payout Rate. Based on current research, I know it is essentially impossible to draw 8%, inflation adjusted, on any kind of investment portfolio for lifetime. So this pension, though small, represents a screaming good deal. We took the payout, even though it doesn't represent much money.

A final consideration in the lump sum vs. payments decision is the financial health of the paying institution, and the reliability of any insurance or guarantee associations behind it. If you have overwhelming reason to believe the institution might become insolvent and unable to pay your pension, you might choose a lump sum instead. That is not an unrealistic fear, given that many private companies, and even a few cities, have gone bankrupt after robbing their pension funds. It seems less likely that a larger entity like a state would have that problem, but who knows? In theory, any governmental entity has the power, and legal obligation, to levy taxes to pay for pension obligations. However, taxpayers in revolt could sue or vote to change those obligations. It's anybody's guess how such a scenario would play out. Your best bet, as always, is to diversify your income and assets so you aren't entirely dependent on any single entity or any one course of future events....

How Much is Future Income Worth?

How can you value a pension, Social Security, or other future income stream such as an annuity?

Pensions, in particular, can be extremely difficult to assess, for a host of reasons. While their value is usually a function of your contributions, it is generally computed using a complicated formula for which those are just one input. This formula can be impacted by your level of compensation, length of service, holding period, others' participation in the plan, and the general economic and political environment. Some of these formulas are bound to change in the future, as the political process copes, or not, with deep and widespread debt. Lastly, the value is complicated by various withdrawal provisions and penalties, such as "certain and continuous" periods and survivor percents, as well as management expenses and fees.

But, reducing a pension to a single number, its *present value*, as best you can, is a handy way to understand its value and relation to your other assets.

Calculating a present value for any future income requires some math, so this could be the point where you consult a financial pro. But the analysis can be performed on any financial calculator, and is usually straightforward. It's especially easy if you'll be receiving a set amount each month.

First, contact the relevant custodian or administrator and collect any and all the information available about your expected benefit: How much will it be? When will it start? How often will you get it? Will it change over time? Is it inflation adjusted? See if they can at least provide you with an estimated periodic benefit (probably monthly) starting at a certain age.

You then get the present value in two steps: (1) Compute the lump sum value of that income stream at the time it begins in the future, possibly your retirement age. (2) Compute the value of that expected future lump sum, now at the present time, some years before your retirement begins.

These calculations require some minimal financial knowledge, an estimate of future interest rates, and access to a financial calculator. If you want to try it yourself, there are many web sites that offer the necessary Present Value and Present Value of an Annuity Calculators. You'll find links on the Resources page at *CanIRetireYet.com*.

One of the trickiest aspects in valuing future sums of money is choosing a reasonable *interest rate*. That amounts to predicting the future, and nobody can do it reliably.

Given that pensions are reliable sources of income, like bonds, one defensible approach is to use an average long-term nominal bond rate of return. This would mean using an interest rate somewhere in the 4% to 6% range to compute the present value of a pension. If you do that, keep in mind that you have not accounted for inflation, and that those future dollars will be worth less than they are now.

Another handy trick for choosing interest rates is to use the yield for Treasury Inflation-Protected Securities (TIPS) with maturities closest to your retirement date, and to your life expectancy. (These can be found at TreasuryDirect.com.) You're basically leveraging the TIPS market to predict a conservative *real* (inflation-adjusted) investment return for your lifetime. If you do this, then you are building inflation into the equation, and the future dollars you compute will be equivalent to current dollars.

The Immediate Annuity Method

If financial calculations aren't your cup of tea, or even if they are, and you want a second opinion, there is another option for valuing a pension or future income stream. It's a very simple and clever approach that is arguably just as accurate, or more so, than what I have described. And it has the added benefit of offloading the financial prognosticating to people who do that for a living, at no cost to you!

What's the trick? Simple. You get a premium quote for an *immediate fixed annuity* that matches the benefit you expect to receive from your pension. (This is a kind of annuity that pays you a fixed amount, right away.) In other words, you go to an insurance company that is in the business of providing annuities, which are essentially private pensions, and you find out how much they would charge to provide lifetime income in an amount exactly equal to your pension. They will crunch the numbers – everything from investment returns to life expectancy – and give you a lump sum, in reverse. That's the amount you'd have to pay in the private market for your same lifetime pension benefit. And it's as good a guess as any for what a pension is "worth."

You can usually get such quotes on the web, free of charge, and without talking to an agent. Two of the best, long-running sources for quoting and comparing immediate annuities are ImmediateAnnuities.com and Vanguard.com.

Can You Count on Social Security?

Despite its nearly 80-year history, and its status as one of the two largest government programs (the other is Medicare), Social Security remains an enigma to many of us. Some say it's going bankrupt and you shouldn't count on receiving anything. Others blindly expect Social Security and other government programs *alone* to care for them in retirement, putting little effort into building their own savings.

The traditional advice that Social Security is one leg of the three-legged retirement stool (the other legs being private pensions and personal savings) is ancient history. Fact is, private pensions are going away, personal savings are minimal on average, and Social Security can easily *become* the stool, depending on the retiree.

Most baby boomers will rely on their Social Security – some more desperately than others – for a steady, inflation-adjusted portion of their retirement income. Nevertheless, it's trendy in some circles, including among some financial advisors, to discount Social Security *completely*. But when you look at the facts for those nearing retirement now, that just isn't realistic. Social Security will be a key part of retirement for most of us.

Which is not to say Social Security isn't in trouble. According to a recent Social Security statement of mine, "the Social Security system is facing serious financial problems, and action is needed soon to make sure the system will be sound…" Can you imagine the panic if similar language appeared on your bank statement?

If you go to the Social Security Administration's Retirement Estimator online, one of the first things you'll read will be that "by 2034, the payroll taxes collected will be enough to pay only about 79 cents for each dollar of scheduled benefits." It's not so much that Social Security is going "broke," in the sense of having *no* money, as it is that the cash coming in from taxes will only be enough to pay about three-fourths of the promised benefits. So even if no changes were made, you'd still be able to collect most of your benefits.

The root issue with Social Security is that it is not actually a *savings* plan, it's an income *transfer* plan from current workers to retired workers. And the demographics of that equation are changing. In the 1950's there were eight or more workers supporting each retiree. Now, and in coming decades, there will only be two or three. That sounds dire. But realize we've already seen a huge decline in workers per retiree over the past five decades, and that didn't end the Social Security system.

Despite the grim financial realities, it is highly likely that Social Security will survive in something similar to its current form. Why? For one thing, as we've just discussed, the system will remain viable for *another couple of decades* even if the politicians do nothing. Also, the changes needed to fix Social Security, though politically unpalatable, are relatively small. Most projections show that modest increases in the payroll tax, or payroll tax cap, or retirement age, would be enough to keep Social Security solvent for decades longer. Those are simple, manageable price tags, compared to the drastic changes needed to address programs such as Medicare.

Given the boomer generation's experience of two stock market busts in just the last decade, it is almost inconceivable that a majority would support removing the guarantees associated with Social Security, and turning the program over to the Wall Street wizards who brought us the Great Recession. Boomers will be a formidable voting bloc in their later years, and would surely overrule any attempts to radically change or gut Social Security.

But, clearly, changes must be made. What form are they likely to take? The reality is that either *taxes* will go up, or *benefits* will be reduced or delayed. The impact of potential tax increases, especially payroll taxes, will probably be muted on today's low- to middle-income near-retirees. The tax burden will fall on younger generations. But, as a potential retiree, it would be wise to plan for the possibility of some modest reduction in Social Security *benefits* down the road.

Reductions could be spread evenly, or as a function of income. In my opinion, because it will be less politically painful, reductions will likely be hidden in the relationship between your benefit and *inflation*. Either the government will change the inflation measurement used for increasing benefits (a proposal is already on the table to use the smaller, but more realistic "Chained CPI"). Or the government will indirectly inflate the money supply faster than the official inflation indexes, so that your benefit dollars will buy less.

Still, I expect Social Security to retain some form of inflation adjuster, giving it a huge advantage over your other income sources. And, as I discussed in *Retiring Sooner*, you have substantial ability to manage your own *personal* inflation rate, and are not entirely at the mercy of the government's inflation index.

Another frequently discussed benefit cut could take the form of an increase in the full retirement age. You might have to wait longer to be eligible for Social Security benefits, and work longer or save more to compensate. Boomers will discover that the Social Security full retirement age has already been gradually increased and is now 67 for anybody born in 1960 or later. Further changes to the retirement age would likely be phased in, and not have a dramatic impact on those near retirement now.

In the end, you must assess the impact of future political changes and future inflation on your Social Security benefits. This is impossible, but we must try. My own, conservative, personal rule of thumb for my early retirement planning was to assume I would receive only **50%** of my projected Social Security benefits. But for somebody nearing retirement now, I don't think it would be unreasonable to assume a portion as high as **75%**. After all, at least that much is projected to be available even if the government does *nothing*.

When to Claim: Hedging Your Bets
The essential tradeoff in claiming your Social Security benefit is that you can get lower benefits starting sooner, or higher benefits starting later – in both cases lasting until the end of your life. There is a crossover age, often around 80,

when it will have made more sense to delay taking benefits, because you'll end up getting more over your lifetime. (That's predicated on your having enough other assets to live on, so that you can delay your Social Security benefit in the first place.)

Virtually all the experts, and all the calculators, show you'll be better off delaying your Social Security benefits as long as possible, up to age 70. Why? Because your benefit is guaranteed to grow faster, and more certainly, than any money you'd save by taking it earlier. Noted retirement researcher Wade Pfau writes, "With an implied payout rate of 9.5%, Social Security *delay* provides a higher payout rate, stronger inflation protection and less credit risk than commercially available annuities."

But I get plenty of pushback from readers on this issue: Many have written to say that, despite all the calculations, it just doesn't "feel" right to delay benefits. They don't trust the government to grow their money, and pay it back later. And, though my engineering brain wants to argue that the logical financial path, the best payoff in the long run, is to delay claiming, I'll confess I share some of those emotional fears!

What if you dutifully draw down your investment portfolio through your 60's, counting on Social Security, and then, just before you become dependent on it, the politicians change the rules?

I don't lie awake at night worrying about the government axing *all* of our Social Security benefits. Still, I think some reductions are likely, so I'm interested in hedging our personal bets. CPA blogger and Social Security expert Mike Piper writes, "a good starting point for planning is to consider a strategy in which the lower earner starts at 62 and the higher earner starts at 70." We currently plan to take his advice: My wife will start her Social Security benefit early, probably at age 62, while I wait as long as possible, up to age 70. With the way Social Security survivor benefits work, since I was the higher earner, this strategy promises to increase the amount we receive as long as *either* of us is alive.

What does that partial early claiming strategy cost us? I've reviewed the leading online Social Security calculators, and they come in handy here. Maximize My Social Security reports about $26K in reduced lifetime benefits, while Social Security Solutions reports about $88K. Doing a rough calculation, that works out to about $200/month in lost retirement income, worst case. Is it worth the peace of mind for us to give up that income each month down the road, in order to definitely get *some* income sooner? Right now, for us, I think the answer is "yes."

Valuing Your Social Security
So Social Security should be around for years in its current form, and probably long after that in something *like* its current form, perhaps with somewhat reduced benefits. It's as foolish to ignore Social Security's potential contribution to your retirement as it would be to rely solely on Social Security's limited payments for your entire income and financial well-being in retirement.

But just how much is Social Security worth to you? How much are you due in the future? What does that equate to in the present? What does that value mean to you?

Here, we'll explore the answers to those questions. I'll discuss how to find your future monthly benefit, as well as show different methods for determining its present value. Finally, I'll explore another reason to be interested in that value – its impact on your asset allocation.

I hope you'll take away one point. *Social Security matters.* It will likely represent a non-trivial portion of the retirement income stream for most of us. Only multi-millionaires can afford to ignore it, and even they might appreciate seeing that government check every month. This is especially true when low interest rates and dividend yields make a predictable, inflation-adjusted income stream significantly more valuable. Social Security is the only such income stream most of us will ever enjoy.

Once you know how much your Social Security is really worth, you can begin to assess how it will contribute to your retired lifestyle, and what other steps you'll need to take to ensure freedom and comfort in your later years.

Make no mistake: Assessing your Social Security benefit is primarily up to *you*. Don't expect the average financial advisor to get very interested in this issue. He or she may even recommend that you "ignore" Social Security. Several I've encountered did that.

Why aren't some advisors interested in helping you understand Social Security? Because, it's not in their interest. Social Security represents a pool of assets that is purposefully *shielded from* the financial services industry, which can't draw management fees or commissions based on what you do with your benefits.

Also, to the extent you receive those benefits, they offset the need for other investment assets. So counting on Social Security is a disincentive to your slaving away to fill the coffers of the financial services industry.

Estimating Your Monthly Benefit
So let's get started assessing your Social Security. First, you need to find out your future monthly benefit. For years the Social Security Administration (SSA) sent out annual paper statements with an estimate of benefits. Then, to save money, the SSA stopped sending out these annual statements in favor of their online calculator. Now it has reinstated the statements online, and on paper for workers age 60 or older. The SSA recommends that everybody go online at least annually, to monitor their benefit records.

Valuing Social Security is easy to start: Just go to the Social Security Administration's site at www.ssa.gov to create an account and retrieve your statement. You will need to enter some identifying data, and can then receive an estimate of your monthly benefit at various retirement ages: 62, full retirement age (67 for me), and 70.

The estimate is based on your earnings during the 35 years when you made the most. By default, the calculations assume that you will continue to work until retirement, making about the same amount as you do now. If you know that won't be the case, you can model different retirement scenarios. The SSA's more advanced calculators are currently located at: www.ssa.gov/planners/benefitcalculators.html.

For more on the Social Security claiming decision, including handy rules of thumb, get Mike Piper's excellent, short, and readable book *Social Security Made Simple*.

Calculating the Present Value

Knowing how much your future Social Security benefit represents to you *today* can help you assess your current savings. Knowing that present value can also help you fine-tune your asset allocation, because Social Security can represent, in essence, a very substantial and conservative holding in your investment portfolio.

So how much is your expected lifetime Social Security benefit stream really worth to you, as a lump sum, in today's dollars? As we learned earlier when discussing pensions and future income, this isn't a simple or precise calculation. It requires some guesses about the future, and must be performed in stages.

First you must value the stream of benefits on your retirement date. That calculation finds the lump sum of money you'd need *at retirement* to generate the expected benefit for the rest of our life. Then you must "discount" that future lump sum into the present, given the number of years until retirement, using some rate of return. The end result is the sum of money you would need now, to duplicate your Social Security benefits in the future.

We won't repeat the details of the calculation here, but you can use the same calculators and assumptions described before. You can also search *CanIRetireYet.com* with the term "Social Security" to find related articles that discuss alternative approaches to valuing Social Security.

Just keep in mind that when attempting to value money decades into the future, your results are likely to be inaccurate. These are imperfect models of an uncertain, distant time. Given the input parameters for my own early retirement scenario, different approaches to valuing Social Security yielded present values in the **low to mid six digits**, differing by about 30%. But that was close enough for my purposes.

Precomputed Values for Social Security
Let's try a generic approach so we can get you some approximate answers quicker....

According to the SSA, the average monthly benefit paid to a retired couple, both receiving benefits, as of late 2015 was $2,670 per month. Let's be conservative and call that $2,500/month. (Note: your benefit depends on your and your spouse's actual work history and retirement ages.)

What would that benefit be worth, compared to your other savings? What lump sum would provide you with $2,500/month (or about $30,000/year) in lifetime income? The initial answer is about $750,000, assuming a 4% safe withdrawal rate. However, if you hope to retire before Social Security age, we have to account for the fact that Social Security doesn't start until sometime in your 60's, possibly later.

So, the table below shows some possible *present values* of Social Security benefits, depending on the years until you reach Social Security age. The calculations assume a real rate of return of 3%, and show what sum of money you'd need invested now, the "present value," in order to generate your expected Social Security benefits in the future. We can conveniently ignore the effects of inflation, since Social Security is inflation-adjusted.

Given that we're attempting to predict a future likely to be filled with economic cycles, political shifts, and a reduction in benefits, I've added a safety factor of 75% in the last column, reducing the total amount. If this seems arbitrary, feel free to choose your own factor, up or down. These numbers represent what Social Security might be "worth" to you, in the present:

Table: Present Value (PV) of Social Security (SS) for Average Working Couple

Years Until SS	Present Value	PV * 75%
0	$750,000	$562,500
5	$646,957	$485,217
10	$558,070	$418,553
15	$481,396	$361,047
20	$415,257	$311,443
25	$358,204	$268,653

The upshot of all these numbers? They let you easily account for Social Security with a simple, ballpark savings number. So, for example, if you are a working couple in your mid 50's now, with about 10 years until you could collect Social Security benefits, you could conservatively add about $419K to your existing retirement savings, to roughly account for the value that Social Security represents in your future. Then you can compare that new sum (your actual savings + $419K representing Social Security) to the total retirement savings thresholds discussed later in the book, to get a quick answer to the question *"Can I retire?"*

(If you use this technique of adding the present value, be certain to remember that you've *already* accounted for Social Security in your current savings – you should *not* factor in any income from Social Security at a later date!)

Should Your Social Security or Pension Affect Your Asset Allocation?

People sometimes ask whether their pensions or Social Security should be considered part of their net worth. For starters, ask whether that value represents an actual vested amount that belongs to you and will pass to your heirs after your death. Social Security and most pensions do not work like that. Since their value won't survive you, don't think of them as an addition to your net worth.

But, since their present value *does* represent income that you can rely on for retirement living expenses, you should definitely consider it part of your income-producing assets. But, should that present value affect your investing strategy or asset allocation?

Various investing and retirement luminaries argue that Social Security or a pension is like a *long-term bond* issued by the government or your former employer, because it pays a very safe and predictable stream of income for a long period of time. Thus, they argue, you can safely increase your allocation to more volatile assets like stocks, to compensate for this large bond that you effectively own. In other words, you can choose to make a given asset allocation more *aggressive*, if you value Social Security and pensions like a bond.

Should you do that?

Here is my experience: I think it's helpful to understand this principle, internalize it, and benefit from whatever peace of mind it offers in relation to your riskier assets. But, having experimented with the idea myself for a few years, I'm against adjusting your asset allocation based on a typical Social Security or pension benefit.

First, as mentioned, this will lead to a more aggressive portfolio – a higher percentage of volatile stocks. And, especially in your later years, and during trying economic times, accounting tricks that lead to a more aggressive portfolio are not advisable for most people, unless they also possess the necessary emotional and financial makeup. Remember that a lump sum from Social Security is *not* going to show on your brokerage statements, to dampen the swings in your investments!

Second, it's simply unconventional to adjust your asset allocation based on Social Security benefits. Though it's theoretically sound, few people actually *do it*, in my experience. Thus, if you choose this route, any time you read about other investment portfolios or compare them to yours, you will be measuring apples against oranges. It will be hard to normalize any published data on asset allocation against your own situation. Typical recommendations and statistics about alternative asset allocations won't apply to you, because you will be making different assumptions from the rest of the world.

So, my advice is to be aware of the present value of your Social Security and pensions, and take their income into account for your budgeting, but, in general, don't let these numbers affect your asset allocation.

Your Investment Portfolio: Income and Growth

Try as you might to design the perfect strategy for retirement income, real life constantly intervenes: The market zigs when you expect it to zag. You have unexpected health expenses, or car or home repairs, or you receive an inheritance....

I've come to view retirement income as something you construct along the way using a bag of proven financial tools, rather than as a single plan or strategy you lay down and follow from the start.

That bag of retirement income tools is diverse. In addition to whatever pension or Social Security you've earned, you have whatever nest egg you've managed to accumulate in an investment portfolio. Most of us will have saved in tax-sheltered vehicles such as IRAs or 401k's, over the years. And the fortunate ones will also have assets in taxable accounts.

When we talk about retirement "savings," we mean the sum of all your investment assets – your income-producing bank accounts, CDs, retirement accounts, stocks/bonds/mutual funds/ETFs, and rental property, less any debts: mortgage, consumer, or other. When exploring potential retirement income, we need to separate assets that produce income from those that don't. For example, your home equity represents an ability to live rent-free, but it doesn't produce income to support your living expenses, unless you rent out a room, or take out a reverse mortgage.

When it comes to your investment assets, there are essentially two ways they can provide for you in retirement: *income* or *growth*. On the income side, your holdings generate dividends in the form of regular payments issued by the underlying companies from their profitable operations. Dividends are appealing to retirees: They appear automatically and are generally, though not always, reliable.

Depending only on the income produced, guarantees your portfolio could survive indefinitely, because you never touch the underlying principal. Previous generations were able to take that approach to investing with ease. But today is different. Even if we are some of the fortunate few who have managed to save adequately for retirement, interest rates and dividend yields can be so low in the current investing climate that it is extremely difficult to live off income alone.

Many people, myself included, are drawn to a dividend-stock strategy for retirement income. The conservative predictability of regular dividend checks is appealing. But the strategy is not perfect: Companies can always reduce or cancel their dividends. And the lack of diversification in a typical dividend-oriented portfolio – which is usually full of utility and financial stocks – could lead to poor performance when those sectors are out of favor.

Your assets can also produce *growth* in the form of higher market prices for your shares. As a historical rule, income has been more predictable than growth, but growth has paid back dramatically during certain time periods. To access that growth, you must liquidate or sell some holdings. This is more complicated than collecting dividends. You must decide *when* to sell, and there are potentially complex tax implications. Also, selling shares is a form of consuming principal, which is repulsive to many traditional retirees. Though, if those shares are growing faster than you are consuming them, your net worth could continue to grow anyway over time.

I started down the passive index investing path years ago. I believe it's more useful to readers for me to follow that path to its end and report on the experience, than it would be to pursue a more esoteric retirement income strategy. The majority of people don't have the time or interest or skills to pursue a dividend stock strategy, while a passive index approach is available to most.

Typically, a passive indexing approach is coupled with a "total return" strategy for retirement income, meaning you draw on dividends *and* growth, when needed to produce retirement income.

I was blessed with rising stock prices in a bull market for the initial years of my own early retirement. That's one of the most beneficial retirement tailwinds you could ask for. But it's not under your control, and it could end at any time. How much will the market drop, and for how long? Nobody knows. What I do know, based on experiencing a number of deep market downturns, is not to change my long-term investment strategy in response.

Given recent high market valuations and low yields, competition for leadership in the world economy, and the historically unprecedented involvement of the Federal Reserve in the U.S. economy, it would be wise not to expect high returns from the stock market going forward. When it comes to long-term stock performance, I tend to knock **2%** off historical returns in my calculations these days. And, unfortunately for all of us, that means needing more in savings to support a given lifestyle in retirement.

The Two Schools of Retirement Income

At retirement, or sometime within the first decade after, you'll have a difficult decision to make. Do you keep your retirement assets in the stock market, where you'll have more flexibility and better odds for long-term financial growth, along with a chance of failure? Or do you go the safe, secure route and *annuitize* your assets for a reliable, though possibly mediocre, retirement paycheck?

Annuities are contracts with an insurance company, purchased for a lump sum, that pay income on a regular schedule. The annuity approach is favored by the "safety-first" school of research, and by the insurance industry. The systematic withdrawal approach is favored by the "probability-based" school of research, and by the investment industry. Insurance types think that market performance is not guaranteed, even over very long time spans, and that systematic withdrawals are needlessly reckless. Investment types think stocks are predictable "for the long run," that they always go up, and annuitizing needlessly leaves money on the table.

Notice the strong correlation between the favored solution and the products being sold. If you're an insurance salesperson, you probably think an annuity is the right approach to retirement income. If you're a stockbroker, you probably think that a systematic withdrawal plan from an investment portfolio is the right approach. Each point of view has its merits, and its drawbacks. What should the rest of us do?

I've been studying the experts on both sides of this issue for years, and I don't think there is a slam-dunk answer. If you've saved very little, then you will probably be forced to annuitize to have any hope of meeting your income needs. If you're very wealthy, then you can probably afford to keep your wealth wholly invested in the markets indefinitely. You can ride out the bumps, while continuing to withdraw at relatively low rates that won't threaten the life of your portfolio.

In my opinion, most of the rest of us will want to adopt a *hybrid* solution – a combination of the two approaches – to get the benefits of both, while hedging our bets against the failure of either. Let's dig into the details of both schools of retirement income....

Probability vs. Safety

The *probability-based* retirement income philosophy generally involves managing an investment portfolio using some type of withdrawal strategy. It could be a fixed "safe" withdrawal rate, or a variable withdrawal rate. The advantages of this approach are its flexibility and its potential upside. Your capital remains under your control at all times. You don't hand it over to somebody else to manage. And, the odds are in your favor over the long term. Data from J.P. Morgan shows that the average long-term return on stocks has been more than 10%. And, in the last 60+ years, the stock market has never gone for *any* 20-year period without delivering at least a 6% profit, annualized.

The disadvantages of this school are significant as well. Most serious but least understood is "sequence of returns risk." Because you aren't simply managing a static portfolio, but must also withdraw to live off it, you are subject to a special *mathematics of loss*. I'll explain this in more detail below, but essentially you must pay the mathematical piper in the form of reduced performance. The next disadvantage is that by relying on a lump sum portfolio for an indefinite period – your lifespan – you are taking on *longevity risk*. The longer you live, the greater the chance that you'll run out of money, regardless of market returns. Finally, if you are managing the money yourself, then cognitive decline could affect your ability to manage your own financial affairs.

By contrast, the *safety-first* retirement income philosophy generally involves purchasing an annuity or bond ladder to "lock in" retirement income. The advantages are security and predictability. You might sleep easier at night knowing you aren't subject to stock market volatility, at least if you have confidence in insurance companies and bond ratings. And your available retirement spending will be known (and fixed) in advance. You won't need to adjust your lifestyle unexpectedly based on future market moves.

But the disadvantages of this school are significant as well. For me, the *single point of failure* looms large: Rather than piggybacking on the self-interest of thousands of companies in the broad stock market, you are trusting a *single insurance company* to look after your interests. *For decades*. Financial planner and commentator <u>Michael Kitces</u> points out that insurance companies *do* fail, and even AAA-rated bonds have measurable default rates. On the other hand, financial planner and researcher <u>Joe Tomlinson</u> makes a strong case that insurers, at least the big top-rated ones, have the financial strength and actuarial prowess to avoid serious problems. He finds only a few cases in history where annuity owners have been shortchanged.

Inflation protection is another question mark hanging over the safety-first approach. It's either unavailable or very expensive in annuity products. So just how "secure" and "predictable" is your safety-first income stream? Add to these negatives the lack of flexibility in managing your money, and no possibility of an upside. You can't generally tap annuitized assets for emergency or legacy purposes. And, if the stock market outperforms other assets – which has always been the case – you will have to watch that party from the sidelines.

Two Styles of Planning

Choosing between the probability-based and safety-first styles of generating retirement income is not just an *investing* decision. It also leads to two different analyses of retirement *expenses*, and two different styles of financial *planning*:

In the probability-based philosophy, you, or a financial planner, lump together all your expenses, essential and discretionary, then compute the *probability* of meeting them over the course of your retirement, using your portfolio of assets. Failure is defined as running out of money before running out of life. A failure probability in the neighborhood of 10% is often considered acceptable. That's *one chance in ten*. So failure is entirely possible, in theory, with this approach. Some people are uncomfortable with that. None of us would get on an airplane with those kinds of odds. But, in reality, complete financial failure is unlikely if the analysis shows a relatively low probability. Why? Because most sensible people are going to *modify their lifestyle* if the numbers start heading in the wrong direction. So the failure rate associated with a probability-based analysis is more a metric for the likelihood and severity of having to adjust your lifestyle, than it is a prediction for the odds of eating cat food later in retirement.

In the safety-first philosophy, you, or a financial planner, *match* guaranteed income to essential expenses. So, if you have non-discretionary expenses that aren't covered by a pension or Social Security, you purchase an annuity, or possibly a bond ladder, to cover that need. In theory, assuming you have enough assets, "failure" is impossible with a safety-first approach. That's because you've assigned guaranteed income sources for all your needs. In reality, there are holes: Those needs won't be fully met unless that income is *inflation-adjusted.* And you are banking that your insurer, and its guarantee association, will remain solvent for decades.

The Most Important Distinction: Risk Management
The financial industry, whether insurance agents or investment advisors, would like you to believe the retirement income debate comes down to security (safety-first) versus upside (probability-based). You are asked to choose between playing it safe or maximizing your retirement lifestyle. In fact, framing the debate that way is a distraction.

Michael Kitces points out, "the real distinction is whether (market and longevity) risk is transferred or retained, and if retained how those risks are managed or avoided."

In other words, the real difference isn't between playing it safe and gambling. There is risk either way. Insurers speak of "risk transfer." In reality, the risk never disappears. It's a question of *who* has the job of monitoring and managing it. So the real difference between the retirement income schools lies in *who* manages the risk – you and your portfolio manager, or an insurance company. And, it should come as no surprise that if you choose to have somebody *else* manage the risk, you'll have to *pay* them to do that job.

As with asset allocation, the most important factor in choosing a retirement income strategy may be understanding which suits your temperament best. Who should manage the risk? You or somebody else? Do-it-yourselfers will likely favor the probability-based approach, and those without financial experience will likely favor safety-first.

Doing It Yourself: Paying for Volatility
Admittedly, do-it-yourselfers have the harder job. If you take it on, you'll need some appreciation for the risk/return of stocks over the long term. I've already referenced a study showing that in the last 60+ years, the stock market has never gone for any 20-year period without turning at least a 6% profit, annualized. But experts can look at the same statistics and come to different conclusions. Some argue that individuals can't rely on averages, because we only get a single chance at retirement. They'll go on to point out that we are in unprecedented market conditions with

low interest rates and high valuations. And they'll say we can't count on historical averages going forward. This is scary stuff, that might send more than a few do-it-yourselfers into the safety-first camp, myself included, at least later in retirement.

Do-it-yourselfers also need a healthy respect for "sequence of returns" risk. This is the mathematical reality that reduces the returns on stocks in a portfolio from which you're taking distributions. In essence, a portfolio that you must withdraw from continually in retirement performs differently from one you can leave alone to accumulate. The problem stems from the impact of those regular withdrawals when the market is down. They rob you of principal that would have provided future earnings.

CFP and professional engineer Jim Otar, in his comprehensive book on retirement planning, *Unveiling the Retirement Myth*, calls this the "time value of fluctuations" (TVF). He offers a formula, based on historical data, to compute its value as a function of the time span. For 20 years, his TVF is about 2.2%. For 30 years it's about 1.6%. So, when living off a portfolio in retirement, at a minimum, you must reduce your expected average long-term stock market returns by at least a percentage point or two, to account for sequence of returns risk.

This volatility penalty sounds like a mark against long-term stock holding, and it is. But it's not a knockout punch. Compare the alternative – annuities backed by a bond portfolio. Bonds, being less risky, are nearly certain to underperform stocks over the long term. And generally bonds underperform stocks by much more than that margin associated with sequence of returns risk.

Finding Your Mix: A Hybrid Approach
Supposedly, if you can't handle a small chance of running low in retirement, then you belong to the "safety-first" camp. If you can roll the dice and still sleep at night, then you are in the "probability-based" school. But that's a simplistic formula for choosing between the two.

The fundamental problem with systematic withdrawal plans is that you cannot fully escape the risk of fatally damaging your portfolio. The fundamental problem with annuities is that you lose control of your money.

That's why I favor a hybrid approach that locks in some essential income from guaranteed annuities, Social Security, and pensions, while leveraging an investment portfolio to provide for an upside of discretionary spending. This balanced approach offers the potential for more spending in the early years of retirement when presumably you are at maximum health and mobility to enjoy it, while guaranteeing lifetime income for essential expenses in later years.

Let's review the advantages and disadvantages of both approaches:

Table: Retirement Income Characteristics

	Probability/Withdrawal	Safety/Annuity
Lifetime income	not guaranteed	yes
Legacy (inheritance)	possibly	usually not
Constant level of income	no	yes
Inflation protection	generally yes	rare and expensive
Upside potential	yes	no
Downside protection	no	yes
One-time/emergency expenses	yes	generally no
Change income as you age	yes	generally no
Maximum payout rate	no	yes
Legal protections for income	not generally	some

These two categories are useful tools for retirement planning. But neither represents the reality of how retirees live their lives. You don't blindly commit your financial success to a single throw of the dice early in retirement. Rather, retirement finances are an ongoing, iterative process.

This is our approach. We are currently treading water in the probability-based pool, and I expect that to continue for another ten years. Then we'll likely pull the trigger on a partial safety-first solution in our 60's, by purchasing annuities with a portion of our assets.

Why are we doing it this way? Generally speaking, the safety-first approach is *irreversible*. Once you buy an annuity, you own that decision for life. The probability-based approach is more flexible. Yes, you must be prepared to cut spending if needed, but you can also take advantage of any upside that appears. In the first half-decade of our retirement, our assets have done a little better than expected, and we have chosen to spend a little more. We have the health to enjoy that spending, and the ability to cut back or generate more income if needed. In later years, our expenses will probably fall naturally. If not, we may need to cut back. We are OK with that. Had we already chosen safety-first and annuitized, we would have locked in a more restricted lifestyle that could have left us regretting the decision in our 50's.

"Probability-based" and "safety-first" are the *extremes* in retirement planning. As in other areas of life, you'd do well to avoid those extremes and find the compromise path that is right for you. Rather than picking sides, many retirees will be best served by diversifying their strategies to create a *hybrid* retirement income solution. Understand your own temperament and finances, then choose your own best mix and timing.

Annuities: Do-It-Yourself Pensions

If you're like many independent-minded investors who cut their teeth on the market conditions of the 1990's, you may harbor serious suspicions about annuity products. Who needs an annuity? With the stock market averaging near double-digit returns in the past, you could easily live off 4%, 5%, even 6% of your portfolio every year, without fear of drawing it down, and even expect that your holdings would grow in the process!

The independent financial press has done much to debunk the complex annuity products offered by the insurance industry. Many variable annuities, and more recently equity-indexed annuities, have been exposed as frightfully complicated contracts, larded with administrative expenses, hidden fund charges, costly riders, and poisonous surrender fees.

Even if one of these opaque products happened to be a fair bargain, it would be extremely difficult to know which one, because they are almost impossible to compare to one another!

Small wonder then that many careful, frugal investors have long ruled out any sort of annuity as a retirement solution. For years, I avoided annuities because of what I read about the expenses and complexity. Why would I need an annuity, when I was enjoying great success at growing my own diversified portfolio, well in excess of our retirement income needs?

But then three events transpired:

1. The market crashed in 2008-2009. Though our portfolio did better than most, and we had no need to produce income at that time, the huge stock market swoon allowed me to see a less-than-rosy picture through the eyes of others who had the ill-fortune to retire at the wrong time. And I knew that those who had purchased annuities, even the overpriced and complicated ones, were very happy with the steady paychecks they received during the crisis. I realized that annuities, of some sort, might have a place, at least for those without the investing skills and fortitude to endure a great recession. And that's a lot of people.

2. I retired. The decades looming ahead of me without a regular paycheck suddenly became very real, in a way they never could until I began the actual experience. It didn't matter that I had many years of investing under my belt, and was confident in my ability to manage our portfolio at least as well as the pros at the large insurance firms. It didn't matter that I was happy living on a budget, and could make additional reductions if needed. Because there was one thing I couldn't control: *how long I would live*. And, ironically, those large insurance firms *could* control for that factor: Simply put, by pooling my lifetime with thousands of others in annuities, they could efficiently insure us all against running out of money.

3. I reviewed my estate plan. I realized that, even though I had done a decent job of saving and providing for my family, in terms of the amount of assets we had accumulated, I had overlooked one

important factor: I had assumed that I would be around to manage those assets for the duration. But what if I weren't in the picture? Was I confident that my loved ones could make that wealth last as needed, regardless of whether they had any interest or skill in investing or money management? I could see they would need at least the option to put a portion of our assets on "autopilot," so they could count on essential lifetime income, free from worries....

In light of these events, I began to see annuities differently, and more positively. Then along came new research demonstrating that adding a simple annuity to a diversified portfolio, or substituting annuities for bonds, might increase safe withdrawal rates and portfolio sustainability.

Given my penchant for diversification, I began to realize it could make sense to diversify my long-term portfolio management strategy by using an annuity for at least some of our assets. I wouldn't do this right away, but as we grew older and had fewer options in life, I could see a more and more compelling case for locking in an income floor.

In general, an annuity lets you create a higher lifetime income stream than you can generate with the same amount in a conventional portfolio of stocks and bonds. This is because, with an annuity, you're consuming both principal and earnings: There is no money left at the end. You are also pooling your lifetime risk with that of other buyers. So the money of those who die first goes to support those who live longer.

I'm talking here about using plain-vanilla single premium immediate annuities (SPIAs), not their complex and expensive cousins – the variable and equity-indexed annuities. With a SPIA you hand the insurance company a lump sum and they immediately begin paying you a monthly amount, no volatility, no indexing, no extra fees. SPIAs are relatively simple products. They are "do-it-yourself" pensions, guaranteeing income for life in exchange for giving up your principal. I'm gradually coming around to viewing these "good" annuities as functioning like another asset class in diversifying a post-retirement portfolio. They remove longevity risk – the chance you'll outlive your assets – from the equation.

Of course immediate annuities, like other kinds of annuities, still have serious limitations:

- They are only as secure as the underlying company and its state guarantee association.
- They reduce your flexibility for meeting large or unplanned expenses.
- They typically eliminate or reduce your ability to leave principal in a bequest to your heirs.
- They generally do not keep up with inflation, or require expensive and imprecise riders to do so.
- Their costs and value fluctuate with interest rates, which are unpredictable over the long term.

So it's important to realize that annuities of any flavor are not a silver-bullet solution for retirement income. They are simply one tool to be used in conjunction with your other retirement income assets. Effectively integrating annuities with an investment portfolio is a complex topic, still under research. But there are a few principles you can keep in mind as you consider retirement planning using annuities:

- Most people, when they really think about it, find unacceptable the prospect of running out of guaranteed lifetime income for essential expenses in retirement. Annuities can fix that problem.
- The cost of using annuities will probably be less "upside" in the later stages of retirement – less opportunity for discretionary spending should the markets do well. But most people are comfortable with living a constrained lifestyle at the end of retirement, as long as they have no regrets about how they were able to live in earlier stages.
- Annuities that incorporate complex provisions or charge anything other than rock-bottom fees rarely compare favorably to other sources of retirement income.
- "Guarantees" by private entities are more like "promises." Overly complex guarantees aren't really a guarantee at all. There is no law guaranteeing that a given insurance company will be in business and able to make good on its commitments 40+ years from now.
- An insurance company cannot outperform the market with your annuity premium, it can only add mortality credits – the transfer of premiums and earnings from those who've died to those still living.

A Floor with an Upside

Could you live off your investment portfolio indefinitely, if you had to? The answer to that question lies in the relationship among your total assets, your living expenses, your investing skill, the length of your retirement, market valuations when you retire, and market performance thereafter. That's a lot of *variables*, only some of which you can control.

My investment results from the two decades before retiring gave me confidence that we could live off our portfolio for the rest of our lives through a variety of economic conditions. We held a conservative but diverse portfolio that had weathered both the 1990's dot-com bust and the 2008-2009 Great Recession. I knew I owned at least one asset class that would perform well in any investment climate, and I had proven to myself under real-world conditions that I wouldn't panic out of the others. *What was there to fear?*

Then I retired and uncovered some sobering statistics. I learned that the odds of depleting even a substantial portfolio were much higher than expected. The math behind a *distribution* portfolio (one where you are making steady withdrawals as markets cycle) is much less forgiving than the math behind an *accumulation* portfolio, where you are saving. When you *withdraw* money in a down market, even a small leg down, you are effectively "locking in" a loss forever, so that portion of your money never has the opportunity to grow again. The results are punishing over the long haul....

In *Unveiling the Retirement Myth*, Jim Otar reports that, even at a low withdrawal rate of 3%, there is nearly a **one in**

four chance that your portfolio will sustain a loss early in your retirement from which *it will never recover*. That doesn't necessarily mean you will run out of money, but it does mean your net worth launches on a steady downward trajectory. I don't know about you, but I don't like those odds!

In *early* retirement, you might choose to live off your portfolio in an ad hoc manner. Many in early retirement will think, *"If my investments begin to underperform, I can always go back to work."* That may be true, but it's wise to be realistic about your options for returning to the work force. Don't expect to bring back your old salary. It's advisable to keep your own personal realities firmly in mind as you plan for retirement income. The point when you can no longer work is a "point of no return" for your investment assets.

Once you are out of options for producing income and growing your assets, then what? The choices are slim and grim: borrow from family, move in with children, take public assistance (SNAP aka "food stamps" requires you to spend down all but about $2,000-$3,000 in assets to qualify), live out of your vehicle. I'm serious! It's not a bad idea to visualize yourself in some of these unpleasant scenarios, to build motivation for what I have to say next....

Once you add up all the factors around retirement income, I've come to believe that you should do everything in your power to create a guaranteed *income floor* for yourself by late retirement (the time period when you cannot reasonably return to work). You want to use every means at hand to assure yourself of a reliable income stream that meets your essential living expenses, from the time you can no longer work until the end of your life, however long that may be.

This process starts by first understanding your *essential living expenses*. This involves some personal choices about what you consider *indispensable*. That is going to be a function of your past lifestyle, your location, your obligations, and your flexibility with respect to your living surroundings. For me, essential expenses allow for a small condo or townhome, food, insurance, medical care, taxes, and utilities. That works out to about 60% of our current retirement budget. The rest is *discretionary* spending, and could be foregone or cut way back if necessary, especially later in retirement.

Next you must add up all the guaranteed, inflation-adjusted sources of income that you can rely on receiving at retirement. Many of us can count on some Social Security. A few can count on pensions. You might also include net income from rental real estate in this figure, plus income from any government inflation-adjusted securities that you intend to hold indefinitely.

Finally, you compare those two values. If your expenses exceed your income, as they will for many, you must "backfill" up to the amount of your essential expenses from a new guaranteed income source. That means you must *annuitize* whatever portion of your nest egg is required to lock in this essential *income floor*. In essence, you will pay a portion of your nest egg to an insurance company (or multiple companies, for diversification), in exchange for a lifetime income stream.

Don't like the idea of parting with some of your nest egg permanently? Many of us will have no choice in order to generate the retirement income we need. But research does suggest that if your uncovered annual expenses are *less than* about 2% to 3% of your assets, you *might* be able to skip the annuitizing step without undue risk. In other words, if you have sufficient assets, and a low enough draw against them, then your portfolio should survive most conceivable economic conditions over most conceivable life spans. But few will fall into this select wealth bracket. And, even if you do, you might still sleep better, and enjoy fewer money management hassles, by purchasing an annuity.

Once you've accepted the need to part with a portion of your nest egg, you can enjoy the benefits of knowing you and your spouse will not want for basic living essentials as long as you live. (Understand that providing for your spouse with an annuity, should you die first, generally requires purchasing an extra-cost rider.)

After you've locked in an income floor, you can apply your time and energy to managing your remaining assets for an *upside*. The balance of your portfolio can stay invested in the market and assume some modest risk, or not, as you choose. (I will continue to hold a diversified, balanced, all-weather portfolio.) You can spend only the *income* from that portfolio, or you can spend some of the *principal* on things, activities, or causes that matter to you. You can be confident you won't be destitute if your portfolio runs out in later years. Because you will have long ago established a baseline of guaranteed income for life.

Working in Retirement

"Retirement" is a relatively new concept. Until midway through the last century, there simply wasn't enough accumulated wealth on the planet to support extended retirement for most human beings. Recently we've experienced a "baby boom" – favorable demographics that allowed for longer and more carefree retirements for the parenting generation. Now the pendulum is swinging back: For the boomers themselves and succeeding generations, "retirement" will have a very different character. It is likely to be longer, more active, more affected by economic and social changes, and integrated with some form of *work*.

"Work" and *"retirement"* would seem to be contradictory terms, but today's retirees, especially early retirees, know that isn't so. CNN Money reports that "70% to 80% of pre-retirees plan to include part-time or some other type of work in their retirement routine." Modern "retirement" is more about having the financial freedom to do the meaningful work that you choose, with income as a secondary concern, than it is about full-time leisure.

That is the real secret to "secure" retirement. The uncomfortable truth is that there are so many variables, so many unknowns about the future, that, unless you are extremely wealthy, there is almost no way to guarantee complete security. A typical retired couple with a prudent lifestyle arguably needs savings of *several* million dollars to eliminate *any chance* of their retirement derailing. Few will achieve that level of wealth. Enjoyable, sustainable part-time work that produces a modest monthly income is a strong asset: Given a 4% withdrawal rate, if you earn just $1,000/month or $12,000/year, that's equivalent to having saved another $300,000 towards retirement! And, it's a lot easier to find a job that produces $1,000/month than it is to save $300,000.

Working in retirement has priceless emotional and social, as well as financial benefits. Creating a product or providing a service that is genuinely useful to others is a proven route to meaning and purpose in life. It can also help you forge rewarding new relationships that are different from those you had when climbing a career ladder. Last, having control over a small extra income stream in retirement is possibly the best tool at your disposal for coping with our personal and collective uncertain futures: surprise expenses, inflation, recession, market gyrations, and so on.

Part-time work that can scale up or down to changing economic conditions, at least in the early years of retirement, removes some of the impossible task of predicting investment returns, inflation rates, government policies, and contingencies, because you can produce some extra income as needed. And, importantly, that income is generally *inflation-adjusted* – because the *value* of most goods and services relative to other goods and services in the economy stays relatively stable, regardless of the actual level of prices assigned to them.

With longer life spans, many of us will have more spare time than we know what to do with. All-day, every-day leisure may not be as rewarding as we are led to believe in glossy retirement ads. Many of us want to keep contributing in meaningful ways, even when we are no longer part of the full-time work force. With some change in perspective, and a few ground rules, you may find that working part-time in retirement is both profitable and enjoyable.

However, working in retirement *is different* than a full-time career. The commitment, pressure, obligations, and rewards, are all less. And that's for the better. Ideally a part-time job in retirement will be something new, creative, and meaningful for you. Without the requirement for a full-time paycheck, you can be more generous with your time and effort. You'll find that people appreciate that. You might even have fun!

While working in retirement is still not the norm, it is on the rise. The Bureau of Labor Statistics reports that the labor force participation rate for seniors nearly doubled from 1990 to 2011. And workers 55 and older logged 42% more part-time hours than they did 10 years previously.

An informal survey on a leading retirement forum posed this question to seasoned retirees: "Were you able to find or create the rewarding part-time work you wanted, when you were ready, without too much stress?" A reassuring 75% of respondents answered "Yes."

In many cases, the work found them: Opportunities for extra income are likely to appear as you pursue your usual interests. Hobbies, volunteer work, and past professional contacts can all produce interesting leads. Without financial pressure, you can bide your time until the right opportunity appears, then say "yes," and give it a try.

What Should You Do?

Perhaps you already have some part-time work in mind, or you could go half-time at your existing job and would enjoy that. Otherwise, give some thought to your options.

Ideally, part-time work in retirement will have a few clear characteristics:

- It will be something you *enjoy* doing, that in no way adds physical or mental stress to your life or feels like "work."

- It will take place on a *flexible* schedule that doesn't compete with other important aspects of your life.

- It will *scale* up or down relatively easily – so you can work more or less, depending on circumstances.

- And, perhaps, it will have a creative or service component that provides *meaning* to your hours, and room for personal growth.

With retirement, you have the opportunity to build up a fun, diverse new skill set that will be useful to you, personally, and possibly lead to opportunities for pay. Be aware and proactive as you go about your daily activities. Many businesses – from amazon.com to the convenience store around the corner – welcome experienced, reliable employees on a part-time basis. You might even pick up work at a store or facility related to a favorite hobby!

If you are more particular about personal freedom and the exact nature of the work, I think *freelancing* is the best route for a profitable part-time gig. You need to find a niche that suits you, where you have an edge. Consider your top skills, strengths, and interests. Think about providing a freelance service that is related to your previous career, or a favorite hobby, or something completely different. Ramit Sethi, "Generation Y's favorite personal finance advisor," is my favorite source for insightful advice on building a freelance business. You can sign up for the first round of his material, free, at Earn1K.com.

There are many web sites for retiree jobs: Resources for older job hunters include SeniorJobBank.org, Workforce50.com, RetiredBrains.com, Encore.org, RetirementJobs.com, and Workamper.com.

In general, I wouldn't recommend *starting* a business to any early retiree whose first priority is *income* – the risk is just too high. I especially wouldn't put all your eggs into one basket by spending much on specialized training, or buying into a franchise. If you do start a business, make *sure* it's one that doesn't put you in debt, and that builds your repertoire of marketable skills.

Finding the perfect work is not always easy, at any stage of life. But it's easier in retirement, when you need less, are more flexible, and can take your time to find the right opportunity. With no pressure to make the big bucks, odds are favorable that you will find work that is a good fit for you.

Why You Need Multiple Sources of Retirement Income

In generating retirement income, you need diversity. There is no single income source ideal for all conditions. Some types of retirement income are good for a lifetime, but lock you into a set cash flow. Some protect against the menace of inflation, but cost more up front. Some maintain flexibility, but expose you to market fluctuations.

The only way to obtain true security in a modern retirement is to generate income from *multiple sources* which, taken together, protect you from the range of financial risks.

In his excellent *Money for Life*, Steve Vernon spells out four goals for retirement income: longevity protection, inflation protection, flexibility for emergencies or inheritance, and minimizing exposure to market risk. To this essential list, I'll add two goals of my own: solvency and simplicity.

Let's explore each of these goals, and the retirement income sources that can achieve them....

Surveys show running out of money is one of retirees' greatest concerns. You need some level of retirement income to last your full lifetime. And yet you don't know how long that will be. Dying early is "good news," financially. But most of us would prefer the "bad news" of living longer. You can look at your personal and family health history and make some rough guesses about your likely life expectancy. But you can't be certain. This is the essential conundrum of retirement planning: How do you generate income for life? Fortunately, there are some answers. The retirement income sources that provide longevity protection by design are annuities, pensions, and Social Security.

Over the decades of retirement, inflation is a serious threat. You have more control over your *personal* rate of inflation than most pundits allow, but you can't ignore its potential effects on a long retirement. At the historical inflation rate of about 3%, the value of your dollars will be cut in *half* in about 23 years. That's a time span that many of us, or our spouses, will live to experience. There are two ways to secure inflation protection in your retirement income. One is through contractual or legal guarantees, like an inflation rider on an annuity policy, or Social Security's annual cost of living increase. The other way to obtain inflation protection is by owning the underlying assets that are inflating in value – businesses (stocks), real estate, commodities – rather than keeping much of your wealth in cash.

The most important lesson of my early retirement so far has been this: "Stay flexible!" Despite careful planning, our financial life has been less than predictable. Our tax returns have been dramatically different each year. Some of the news has been good: an inheritance, modest income from my blog. Some of the news has been bad: medical bills, car repairs, travel expenses. Even though we are currently in our ideal retirement location, our feelings or needs could change, and we could move on. That would be an expense. Like many, we want to pass on assets to worthy causes and the next generation when we die. That requires not locking all our wealth up in annuity contracts. How do you retain maximum flexibility in retirement income? The answer is simple: maintain a *balanced, liquid portfolio* of stocks, bonds, and cash.

Unfortunately, stocks entail market risk. Prices fluctuate based on supply and demand and the economic cycle. For experienced, long-term savers this is not a problem. It comes with the territory of investing. But, in retirement, when you must draw on your assets for income, when you must factor in an uncertain lifespan, when you may be battling physical or mental decline, volatile assets are a serious issue. You can't necessarily wait out a market downturn in your 80's or 90's. The traditional income sources that insulate you from exposure to market volatility are *fixed income*: bonds, CDs, bank savings. And people often think of these kinds of assets as "safe." Yet they are *not* safe from longevity risk or inflation. Annuities and Social Security are safer still. They potentially protect against three risks – longevity, inflation, and market exposure. But, with them, you lose flexibility. There is no access to your principal.

And, with annuities, in the worst case, there is solvency risk. Annuities are sold as a sure thing, an asset no different from owning a business or real estate. But, in fact, an annuity is a contract with an insurance company. You are betting that company will stay in business to make regular income payments for decades. Under normal conditions that should not be a problem: Insurers are heavily regulated and insured, and most are highly profitable. But we aren't just concerned with "normal" conditions here. Under normal conditions you can also put all your money in a broad-based stock index fund and come out *way ahead* of most other potential retirement income sources. It's when economic conditions are abnormally bad that we need to be especially concerned about solvency. And I'm not convinced that insurance companies would be any better off than the rest of us. If the economy is so weak that a diversified investment portfolio is permanently damaged, can we be certain that insurance company payments wouldn't be affected?

The federal government may be marginally better off than insurance companies in a prolonged downturn. It can "create" money, after all, at the price of inflation. But, without changes, Social Security will be insolvent in less than two decades. Bottom line: The portions of your retirement income that depend on private or public pensions are only as good as the institutions standing behind them. At some level, almost no retirement income source is free from solvency risk. But your risk is lower anywhere there is less *bureaucracy*. The more *directly* you own your assets – living on your own fully paid up farmland would be the ideal – the less chance you will be affected by somebody else's bankruptcy.

The final goal for retirement income is simplicity. Many seem to think that financial success is about technical sophistication, or gaming the system. But my experience says the opposite: Wealth building is about transparency and simplicity. Spend less than you make, grow the savings, and don't lose it. It's much easier to accomplish this if you *minimize the moving parts*. The often-unseen risk of complexity is that you may not be getting what you think you are. And that's truer than ever in retirement, when you are less and less able or inclined to manage exotic financial assets. What's the simplest way to maintain simplicity? Reduce the *number* of your financial holdings, and reduce their *cost*. High expenses typically mean high complexity, low returns, and bad news....

Financial security in your later years requires meeting the competing goals of longevity protection, inflation protection, flexibility, reduced volatility, solvency, and simplicity. Given that no single retirement income source achieves all of those goals on its own, you will need more than one.

For maximum security, most retirees will want one income stream that is market-based (stocks), one that is insurance-based (annuity), and one that is socially based (pension or Social Security). With those three types of income in place, you will be prepared for any kind of retirement weather....

Take Action

- If you expect a pension, collect all the relevant information about your benefits from the administrator and assess its value to you.
- Choose a simple financial calculator and try out some simple approaches for valuing future income.
- Log in to the Social Security Administration web site and review your statement of benefits. If you expect your work situation to change significantly between now and retirement, use one of the more advanced SSA calculators to estimate your benefits.
- Compute or estimate the *present value* of your Social Security benefit.
- Review the asset allocation and yield of your investment portfolio: Do you have an income or growth-focused strategy?
- Explore the web sites for immediate annuities, and get some trial quotes for a portion of your current investment portfolio.
- Just for fun, brainstorm some potential part-time retirement "jobs" for yourself. Entertain *only* the options that are fun, rewarding and interesting to you.

3: RETIREMENT MATH: A PRIMER

"As far as the laws of mathematics refer to reality, they are not certain; and as far as they are certain, they do not refer to reality." — Albert Einstein

Now that we've explored your income and expenses – the detailed input to the retirement question – let's take a high-level look at the basic math behind all retirement analysis. We'll look at the essential equation involved, and its variables. But, don't worry, the math required is very simple, even if the judgment calls are not!

In case you're feeling overwhelmed by the financial planning task ahead, we'll consider the pros and cons of hiring a financial advisor. Spoiler alert: I think most people, most of the time, can do a better job themselves!

Next, we'll explore your most essential tool for planning your own retirement: retirement calculation software. We'll discover why even the best retirement calculators cannot provide precise answers. We'll also review my extensive surveys of the field of available retirement calculators, to identify which ones are right for you.

By the end of this section, you'll have learned your way around the basic retirement equation and the many available tools for calculating it. You will be familiar with the important retirement input variables and with Monte Carlo, historical, and average return simulations. You'll also understand the differences in retirement calculator *fidelity*.

Then, with a basic understanding of retirement math and tools, you'll be empowered to crunch your own numbers and draw your own conclusions about the state of your financial affairs....

Understanding the Two Sides of the Retirement Equation

It's enough to make even a number-loving engineer **dizzy**: *savings, expenses, interest rates, investment returns, inflation rates, tax rates, safe withdrawal rates....*

What are we talking about? The *retirement equation*: the essential relationships between all the variables that determine how long your money will last into the future. Fortunes are made by calculating, prognosticating about, and manipulating this formula.

But, despite all the words uttered and pixels consumed on behalf of this equation, it actually boils down to a simple relationship that anybody can understand:

(Your Savings) x (Estimates About the Future) ==> Income for Future Expenses

Putting this into even plainer English: all of your *savings* – cash, investments, retirement accounts, annuities, pensions, Social Security – go into a pot at the time you retire. Then you, or a financial advisor, or an insurance company, apply some *estimates or predictions* about what will happen in the future to that pot.

Those predictions about the future determine the *rate or multiplier* to use for withdrawing from your savings. Based on that rate, you take from your savings pot some amount of *income* each month to pay your living expenses. In a nutshell, that's the retirement equation.

Note there are two sides to the equation: savings on the *left*, income or expenses on the *right*. As you approach and reach retirement, and long afterwards, you will be extremely interested in the right-hand portions of this equation – estimates about the future, and income.

But, long before you can think in those terms, you will have been focused on the *savings* part of the equation. That's the part that you can track and influence during your working years, to create a better retirement for yourself. In *Retiring Sooner*, I recommend tracking that savings (or net worth) number starting as early as possible in your career, so that you get regular feedback on whether your spending and saving habits are leading you in the right direction, or not.

That savings number is critical for retirement planning too: It helps you see the big picture retirement equation, before introducing the complexities of future income and cash flow. But there is a catch: Many retirees have assets that don't easily reduce to a single "savings" number – a pension, annuity, or Social Security – for example.

In section 2, we explored techniques for handling that situation, lumping assets into your savings via simple addition of *present values*. The advantage is that you end up with a *single* "equivalent" number for each asset, which you can add to your savings on the left side of the retirement equation above. This can simplify both tracking your progress against your goals while working, and figuring out if you'll have enough to support yourself after you retire.

The Three Unknowns That Dominate Your Retirement Equation

Retirement calculators are supposed to make retirement-related decisions easier, showing you how much you need to save, or how much you might be able to spend once you reach retirement. But as soon as you open up one of these tools you are plunged into a confusing world of abstract mathematical variables. One of the most common problems people have is simply knowing what data to enter!

And there are *three unknowns* that dwarf all the others. These are absolutely essential for performing any retirement calculation, and yet nobody *else* can really tell you what they should be. You can pay an advisor to make some educated guesses. But what you're really buying is his or her *personal* views about the environment, politics, and your health. That's right, when you really dig into these supposedly precise mathematical values, you'll find yourself facing some unexpectedly subjective judgment calls on some surprisingly emotional topics....

The growth rate. We've all heard that the long-term historical return from the stock market is in the neighborhood of 10%. Yet in recent years we've seen a steady stream of news and views questioning whether we'll ever get those returns again. What underlies the growth of stocks? Simply this: the growth in the *economy*. And how has the economy been doing over the long term? In the 1950's and 60's real growth in Gross Domestic Product (GDP) averaged about 4% annually. In the 1970's, 80's, and 90's it averaged about 3%. And since 2000, the average growth in GDP has dropped under 2%. What's causing that decline in growth?

Growth requires *consumption*. So if growth is limited, it's probably because we're running out of something. What could we be running out of? Fuel, land, other natural resources? Your answer, and your beliefs about how long we can sustain our current consumption patterns, will determine what values you use for the growth of your investment portfolio.

The inflation rate. Since the 1970's, when it averaged slightly over 7%, to today, when it's lurking under 2%, the officially stated inflation rate has been in a long-term decline – though we've seen some volatility and spikes along the way. Inflation is defined as the percentage rate of increase in the prices of goods and services (or the decrease in the value of the dollar) in the economy. In one possible mathematical analysis, inflation can simply be subtracted from your investment return, so it is a headwind to the growth of your portfolio and its ability to support you.

As I explained in section 1, inflation is a back-door tax on wealth, a mechanism for the government to spend money it doesn't have, by taking wealth from those with savings and giving it to those who borrow. Whether or not you approve of that policy is a political matter, but the mechanism itself is pure economics. So what might inflation do in the future? Nobody knows. But your answer to that question is probably dictated by your views on whether there will be more or less government involvement in the economy going forward. And the impact on you, personally, will depend on where you sit on the wealth scale, compared to your neighbors. If you're better off, you'll probably lose out from increases in inflation, and if you're less well off, you're likely to gain.

Your life span. The final unknown factor that dominates your retirement calculation is simply the length of your life. We'll all know the date when our retirement starts. And we all know we must leave this world at some point. But none of us knows exactly when. Since the 1950's, average life expectancy at birth in the United States has risen from approximately 65 to about 80 years. Yet this is one area where we all intuitively understand that statistics have little bearing on our personal experience. Genetics, accidents, lifestyle, and health care are just some of the personal factors that could cause our life expectancy to deviate substantially from the average.

How long will you live? Nobody knows. The question is impossible to answer, most of the time. And yet virtually every retirement calculator demands to know how long your retirement will last. To be on the safe side, most of us will plan to live into our 90's or 100's. But, while family history may be a guide, it's still a guess.

So, when we analyze the retirement equation, and when we attempt to compute it using available retirement calculators, we will run up against these three unknown factors: *growth*, *inflation*, and *life span*.

Over the course of little more than a decade or two, modest and entirely plausible changes in any one of these factors could either magnify your retirement savings several-fold, or lay it to waste.

Growth rate. Inflation rate. Life span. How do you know what they will be for you? *You don't.*

Then, how do you calibrate them for yourself within the range of historical and statistical possibilities? Here are where those numbers ultimately come from:

- **Growth rate** comes from your views on the world economy and the *physical* environment it operates within.

- **Inflation rate** comes from your views on the direction of the *political* environment.

- **Life span** comes from your understanding of your own *personal* environment.

Do You Need a Financial Advisor?

We are now at a critical juncture. You've thought through your retirement expenses and income. You've been introduced to the basic math principles underlying retirement analysis. Where do you go from here? Can you proceed on your own, or do you need help? I'm a strong believer in *do-it-yourself* retirement. I think most people have the ability, if they can invest the time. But I don't discount the value of professional advice in all situations....

Given all the variables in the retirement equation and your personal situation, you might be inclined to seek expert advice. And, if you are truly bad with numbers or financial discipline, or have a very complex financial situation, an expert might be advisable.

But understand that many financial advisors are more expert in how to *sell* financial products and conform to the thicket of government regulations for their work, than they are technical experts on retirement finance. And their focus is necessarily on their own livelihood.

I've met advisors who had never run the retirement calculator on their own company site, and others who tell clients to focus on their "feelings" and let the numbers take care of themselves. I've seen serious mistakes made in retirement calculations, from ignoring Social Security, to forgetting to index it for inflation, to using excessive tax rates.

And, if an advisor makes an error in judgment, you can bet it will be on the *conservative* side. Maybe that sounds good, but it means you will be working longer before you retire, and the advisor will be getting more of your assets to manage, and charge fees against, for longer. Several advisors have told me that "compliance runs the show" – the legal department is in charge. As an advisor, it's far easier to get sued for *losing* client assets, than it is for excessively *holding on* to them, whether or not that serves the client.…

Many forms of financial planning or investment management boil down to attempts to predict the future. Smart people and resourceful organizations develop clever models that help them market themselves as having an edge over the competition. But guess what? They don't know the future any better than you do. You pay a lot for certainty, a confident opinion. But that doesn't mean it's correct.

An article on _Advisor Perspectives_ reports on new and old research into whether "experts" can predict the future. One study analyzed 28,000 expert forecasts from a broad variety of domains. On average, the expert opinions were *less accurate than random guessing*. Another study analyzed 6,459 market forecasts from financial gurus over 14 years. The average expert's accuracy in predicting the direction of the market was about 47%. That's *worse than flipping a coin*. The statistical evidence is overwhelming: Nobody can predict the future.

After many years of reading every investment book I could get my hands on, talking to numerous players inside and outside of financial services, making my own mistakes in the real world, and enduring several major market meltdowns, I've learned to simply *accept the uncertainty*.

Aside from predicting the future, I think it's extremely difficult to find an unbiased opinion on *whether or not you can retire*. Even the best financial professionals will have a conflict of interest in trying to answer this question accurately. If they are *commission*-based, they have products they must sell to make a living: They might benefit if you retire sooner and buy an annuity. If they are *fee*-based, then they profit when your assets under management grow: They might benefit if you work longer, accumulating more assets to be managed. And, always, the risk to them is lower if you don't leave your secure job based on their advice.

Still, there are certain money or tax management topics that can benefit from expert advice – the timing of Social Security, integrating annuities with other assets, sequencing and taxation of retirement withdrawals. But know that there are authoritative web sites and powerful software tools available for the do-it-yourselfer in all those areas.

If I, or a family member, absolutely required professional financial advice, I'd start with the advisors at my most trusted, consumer-oriented companies: Vanguard or USAA. If I needed to find a local advisor, I'd use the directories at the NAPFA or Garrett Planning Network sites.

And, once I'd found an individual, I'd have *four questions* for them before turning over my money:

1. Are you bound to a *fiduciary* standard?
2. Are there restrictions on the investment/insurance products you can recommend to me?
3. How are you paid, and at what rates?

4.   Will you put all of this in writing?

You don't need an advisor to predict the future. Financial plans quickly become outdated and are ignored or thrown away. Sophisticated and complex attempts to forecast the future are no better than simple rules of thumb, and possibly worse, for obscuring the view.

But sound financial *behavior* and habits, along with up-to-date *information,* are essential. A good advisor could help coach or inform you in certain situations.

Financial planning should be more about equipping yourself with the tools and mindset for a safe and enjoyable journey, than about trying to predict and control your exact route and arrival time!

Choosing a Retirement Calculator

Just because you don't rely on a professional advisor, doesn't mean you'll ignore outside expertise in your retirement planning. When it comes to actually evaluating the retirement equation for *your* specific retirement, you will probably want the help of a *retirement calculator*. These are the most important tools as you prepare for and reach retirement. Thoughtful individuals using a good retirement calculator can know as much about their retirement trajectory as any financial advisor.

Such calculators are plentiful. Use them. Use more than one. But use them with caution.

As software, all retirement calculators can have problems. Not infrequently, I've painstakingly entered my numbers, pressed "Calculate," and watched as obviously nonsensical results were produced. Problems I've experienced when using retirement calculators include bugs in asset allocation, overly conservative tax rate assumptions, inaccurate Social Security assumptions, spurious expenses, errors in date math, rigid data input for near-retirement scenarios, limitations in summary/detail reports, and confusing user interfaces.

But, the *real* problems with most retirement calculators are theoretical, and go deeper....

Refining the Analysis

Let's start with some simple *division*. Say you're retiring at age 65, you've saved $500,000 in your 401k, and you need about $30,000/year to live on, in addition to whatever pension or Social Security you'll receive. (These are made-up numbers; feel free to use your own.) So we divide $500,000 by $30,000/year and see that your money will last about 17 years, until you are age 82.

That simplistic analysis sounds a little tight. What if you live longer?

Maybe we can refine the analysis. Haven't stocks averaged about 10% growth annually? Let's put in a growth factor: so we have $500,000 growing at 10% annually. That's $50,000/year in income. With only $30,000/year in living expenses, your portfolio will last forever! Sounds great.

It's also still *wrong*. For starters, we forgot about inflation. Let's call that 3.5%, a bit more than the historical average, considering what the government is up to right now.

We also forgot that your whole portfolio probably isn't in stocks growing at 10%. Let's say your *combined* portfolio of stocks and bonds grows at 7.5% annually. (Expecting such growth rates going forward may be delusional, but that's another discussion.)

So, let's run those numbers again: $500,000 growing at 7.5% minus 3.5% (4% real return) annually, less $30,000/year in living expenses. OK, that lasts about 28 years, getting you into your early 90's from age 65. As long as none of your forebears were centenarians, you'll probably be all right....

Or will you? As we'll soon see, this simple, familiar kind of calculation gives you a bit of insight into where you stand financially today. *But it tells you nothing certain about what will happen in the future.*

Modeling Volatility: Monte Carlo Simulations

The simple formula above is essentially the one you'll find in many low-fidelity retirement calculators. But this calculation is flawed as a predictive tool. There are many reasons why. But let's start with this one: It completely ignores the *sequence of investment returns*. It assumes that *average returns* are all that matter.

They aren't. As we've discussed, there is a mathematical penalty for *volatility*. For example, you can easily run out of money in a stock market that returns 10% annually, on average – if those returns *start* below average, and don't increase until too late in your retirement!

Most low-fidelity retirement calculators assume *steady growth* rates, year in and year out. But that's not how the economy or your money works. When you are adding to, and especially when you are withdrawing from, a portfolio, deeper mathematical analysis shows that you will wind up with dramatically different sums, depending on the *order* in which returns, or losses, accumulate.

Higher-fidelity calculators try to model the fluctuations of the markets by incorporating "Monte Carlo" algorithms into their calculations. (The name is a reference to the famous European casino.) These simulations require you to input statistical measures of the *range* of possible values for important parameters like inflation and investment returns. The calculator then picks random values from those ranges, combining them into hundreds, thousands, even millions, of variations.

Surely that will cover all the possibilities? Well, the output data is definitely impressive: You may have seen one of the resulting net worth versus time graphs, bursting with scenario lines, a veritable financial Medusa....

But while Monte Carlo simulations *do* have some value in showing you the outlying *envelope* of possible paths to your future, their fatal flaw is that *the vast majority of those paths are very unlikely!*

It turns out that markets aren't actually completely random, and the randomness they *do* exhibit is not the kind of randomness most often used in Monte Carlo calculators:

Markets actually operate in *cycles* of varying lengths, unpredictable at first, but recognizable over time. So stacking a bunch of totally random factors on top of each other in a Monte Carlo analysis doesn't make for a realistic simulation. The fatal flaw with these calculators is that they introduce *too much randomness*, ignoring long-term trends.

Historical Simulations

So if steady growth and Monte Carlo-based simulations are both misleading, what about using actual *market history*? Some leading financial thinkers have argued that this is the most realistic way to simulate retirements. After all, if your portfolio could have survived the financial events of the past 100 years, shouldn't you be able to rest easy about your upcoming 30- to 40-year retirement?

An approach based on market history has many strong adherents. But while it is better than some of the alternatives, there are still serious flaws. For starters, it assumes that the future will be like the past....

History may rhyme, but it doesn't precisely repeat itself. If we have no other choice, we can plan based on past experience. But, deep inside, we know that the future will turn out differently. The modern world, with its complex technological, financial, and social systems, has the potential for chaotic behavior. Who can really say we've already seen the best or worst possible outcomes?

More Variables

Also, an approach based on market history ignores *current market valuations*. Practically speaking, if you're going to predict the future based on the past, you should at least take into account your starting point. That's why market valuations matter. Researcher Wade Pfau has used historical return data to show that safe withdrawal rates for portfolios are highly correlated to the level of the stock market *at the time of retirement*. (Note: a "safe withdrawal rate" is a hypothetical percentage of your portfolio you could withdraw each year without risk of running out of money over the course of a long retirement.)

Another difficult aspect of retirement calculations is choosing a *life expectancy*. Any retirement calculation that requires you to know the exact time of your death is, by definition, an abstract, academic exercise. That's fine for insurance companies, which can rely on the laws of statistics governing large groups of people, but it's unreliable for an individual.

As you pursue more accurate or sophisticated models of the future, which we'll try in later sections of the book, it should be with a healthy dose of realism. In the end, no retirement calculator can predict the future. All it can tell you is *which direction you're headed*. A calculator can tell you which way to steer, but it can't tell you with any precision where or when you'll arrive.

Still, the best calculators are worth consulting for this reason: They'll give you enough warning to make course corrections before you *drive over a cliff* – run out of money, that is.

The Best Retirement Calculators

Retirement calculators are critical tools and they are not all the same. The distinctions are important because either you, or a financial planner, will use the results from a retirement calculator to make one of the most crucial decisions of your life: *Are you financially independent yet, or not?*

If you get this decision right, you can enjoy more of the freedom and fulfillment that everybody wants out of life. But, if you get this decision wrong, you could run out of money for essentials in your old age, or you could waste years of your life doing unnecessary or unenjoyable work.

Because retirement calculators are so important for life planning, and because I'm a software engineer with a background in numerical modeling, I've searched far and wide for the best tools:

Selection Criteria

- I favored general-purpose tools that take a set of financial inputs and model them over time – suitable for traditional pre- and post-retirement, or early-retirement scenarios.

- I was looking for something beyond trivial time-value-of-money analysis: Each calculator needs to offer some unique value – either in its user interface, its approach, or its analytical power.

- I excluded overly simplistic tools intended for those with no financial experience at all.

- I did not include tools targeted at professional advisors (with price tags to suit), or tools that were obvious loss leaders for other bundled financial services (conflict of interest), or tools that were highly technical or research-oriented.

- I gave weight to reputation and precedent. In general, I wanted to see established companies or experienced individuals who could support their tools with ongoing development, and an established user base, if possible.

I have evaluated almost 100 retirement calculators now, in some form, and worked with many of them extensively. However, I do not generally attempt to *verify their results* mathematically. There are simply too many variables involved and too many judgment calls on the part of programmers for me to issue an opinion that a given calculator is "right" or "wrong." Any calculator, in any given scenario, can be caught making some simplifying assumption about reality that somebody will argue is incorrect. I don't want to play that game.

But, do realize that, in an attempt to make retirement modeling easier, some calculators make assumptions that may not suit your situation. For example, a surprising number of calculators have problems with the *dates* in early retirement and near-retirement scenarios. Also, beware of calculators that require you to input a salary, or want to compute your expenses as some percent of your salary, or assume that Social Security must start at your "retirement" date, or that include built-in and undocumented assumptions for stock market returns, inflation, or tax rates.

Rather than expecting perfection out of any single software program, I suggest getting a "second opinion." You can easily check your analysis by running more than one calculator. There are enough good ones listed here and on my blog, that you can easily get a second or third opinion on your retirement situation.

Key Parameters

Fidelity: I categorize retirement calculators into three levels of "fidelity." (Credit to Stuart Matthews of Pralana Consulting for this helpful concept.) By *fidelity* we are referring to how well each calculator can potentially reproduce reality – the realism of its simulation. To do a better modeling job, a calculator will need to collect more data, and more accurate data, from you. So, "fidelity" is also a rough measure of increasing complexity:

- *Low-Fidelity* — These calculators will feature just a dozen input fields or less, and usually perform only a simple fixed rate/average return calculation. They feature ease of use, and generally will require less than 5 minutes of your time to produce answers.

- *Medium-Fidelity* — These calculators add additional fields, usually handling multiple accounts with different asset allocations, and arbitrary financial "events" such as irregular future income or expenses. Generally, they might require 10-20 minutes of your time to produce answers.

- *High-Fidelity* — These calculators will add even more input fields, the ability to compare scenarios, and Social Security and detailed tax calculations.

Generally, they will require at least 30-60 minutes of your time to produce answers. And they could easily require several hours for you to understand all the options, and collect and input all the data to take full advantage of their capabilities. But these calculators have the potential to be most accurate, assuming you take the time to enter good data, and assuming your guesses about the future hold true.

Returns: Broadly speaking, there are three approaches to modeling stock market returns over time:

- Using an *average* return for each year is the simplest approach. However, unless you reduce that average return by some arbitrary amount, it does not take into account the impact of *volatility* on your portfolio, and will be overly optimistic.

- A *Monte Carlo* analysis, using an average return plus a standard deviation, takes volatility into account, but requires expertise (or trust) for choosing the necessary mathematical parameters. And the mathematical randomness introduced by a Monte Carlo simulation is artificial, and doesn't mimic the real world precisely.

- Finally, a *historical* analysis uses actual market data on the performance of asset classes over the past century to model what would have happened to your portfolio over periods in the past. The criticism of this approach is that the future may not be like the past, or that the current starting point of high market valuations could lead predominantly into the realm of lower return possibilities.

There are recognized experts with arguments for and against each approach to modeling returns. My own preference is to gather as much information as possible, by using calculators that offer all three algorithms, then compare the results and draw my own conclusions.

Platform: The majority of modern retirement calculators run in your browser as web applications. If you want the slickest user experience, you'll probably opt for one of these. A few calculators run on your desktop or mobile device, using Microsoft Excel, iOS, Android, or Windows. If you'd rather keep your financial data on your local device or computer, you might opt for one of those.

Cost: Many retirement calculators are *free*, including good ones at each fidelity level. In general, even the paid calculators offer free versions, so you can try before you buy. A few calculators are offered in different fidelities at different price points. The very best financial planning software for personal use is generally priced from $100-$200. That is a tiny sum compared to the personal and financial magnitude of the decisions involved.

Notes/Features: On <u>my blog</u> you'll find tables with detailed notes on the features of each program I've reviewed. Some valuable features to look for include: dedicated fields for a spouse's data as well as your own; arbitrary incoming or outgoing cash flows; scenario capabilities for comparing financial alternatives; and detailed tax calculations that go beyond simple *effective* tax rates to use *marginal* rates.

Choosing a Calculator

As noted, p*rice* should not be an issue: There are free calculators available at all fidelity levels. If you have a preferred *platform*, that may help filter your list. Most importantly, decide how *accurate* an answer you need, and how much *time* you want to invest in getting it....

If you just want a simple answer to whether your savings are roughly on track to retire in a certain time frame, you should start with the *low-fidelity* calculators to get quick results.

If you want to fine-tune the output more to your specific situation, perhaps looking at how your mixture of assets and future financial events will impact your wealth, start with the *medium-fidelity* calculators.

If you have substantial assets and need to fine-tune a tax or withdrawal strategy in retirement, or you want to model a range of future life events and compare alternative courses of action, use a *high-fidelity* calculator.

In any case, you'll want to try more than one calculator, to confirm your results. For the low-fidelity calculators, I'd run *three* programs before drawing any conclusions, because they are so simple and easy to use. For the medium-fidelity calculators, I'd choose at least *two* programs. You can become proficient in both without a big time commitment. If you need a high-fidelity calculator, I would review the field of choices, then become expert with the one that makes most sense to you. After that, I'd choose a medium-fidelity calculator to rough-check results.

Recommended Calculators for Near-Retirees

I've used many retirement calculators. I relied on these tools to plan my own retirement trajectory. Then I started a blog and began *reviewing* retirement calculators. Over time, those posts have become the most popular on my site.

Despite their shortcomings, retirement calculators are *essential* tools in preparing to leave a career. Nobody, not even a highly compensated financial advisor, can foretell the future. Projections from a retirement calculator are the best we've got. Just remember, a good retirement calculator is a set of *binoculars*, not an *autopilot*. It will give you some visibility into the future, but you still have to drive yourself there....

Retirement calculators come in all flavors. There are tools with sleek, dynamic web interfaces. And there are spreadsheet-based calculators with dowdy, tabular interfaces perfect for geeks. There are simple, fast tools that will analyze your retirement savings in a few minutes. And there are sophisticated personal financial models that will attempt to optimize your retirement withdrawals decades from now.

I've reviewed all types on my blog. But, after all the years, all the reviews, and all the number crunching, I find myself returning to a small subset of favorite high-fidelity financial planners. These are the *"best of the best"* when I need to perform detailed financial modeling. When you're ready to dive deeper into your own financial picture, perhaps one of these will be perfect for you too. Here they are, in the order I discovered them:

J&L Financial Planner

Sometime in the early 2000's, shortly after the idea of early retirement lodged in my head, I started writing a simple computer program to model our personal cash flow into the future. As the job got more complex, I decided to look around and see what other retirement modeling tools were available. At that time there was precisely one candidate that met my needs: the J&L Financial Planner.

Now, more than ten years later, it's still a powerful and competitive tool. More often than not, when I need to model a retirement problem, I turn to the J&L Financial Planner first. For me, it has the most logical and optimal internal architecture for financial modeling. That means powerful and flexible account and event systems. And it offers superb traceability of results, logging *every* individual cash flow in every year of the simulation, so you can easily verify its calculations.

The J&L Financial Planner is available for Windows only. It performs average, historical, and Monte Carlo simulations, though its approach to historical simulations is offbeat. Surprisingly, for such a powerful tool, it doesn't perform detailed marginal tax calculations. Otherwise, it offers just about every possible retirement modeling feature you can imagine. Sometimes those features are buried in the 1990's-era Windows user interface. But, with a little time invested, there are virtually no retirement scenarios you can't model accurately with the J&L Financial Planner.

Flexible Retirement Planner

Not long after starting my blog, I came across a single high-fidelity tool friendly enough that I could recommend it to anyone who wanted to do their own in-depth financial planning. The Flexible Retirement Planner impresses with its simple, clean, and professional user interface, married to a sophisticated financial model. For years, when I thought of the ideal interface for financial modeling, I looked to the Flexible Retirement Planner first. That it is offered freely for non-commercial use, runs on the web and major desktop platforms, and comes with excellent documentation, are added bonuses.

Originally offered only on the web, the Flexible Retirement Planner is now available in download versions for the desktop. Its use of Java can sometimes lead to configuration issues, but once the software is running, it is generally an easy and reliable tool to use.

The Flexible Retirement Planner is a near-perfect mix of simplicity and power. It starts with one input screen, where you can quickly generate results, but offers flexible financial events and simulation options under the hood. It also has very attractive and well-organized graphical and tabular output.

The Flexible Retirement Planner is missing historical simulations, but offers Monte Carlo by default, which can also be configured for average return. It was one of the first calculators to offer variable spending policies.

The Flexible Retirement Planner remains a finely crafted and well-balanced tool. It is mature software now, and development has slowed. However, thanks to its simple, general design, I expect it to remain a viable planning tool for years to come.

Pralana Bronze/Silver/Gold

Some years ago, I received a letter from a retired electrical engineer who, it soon became apparent, might be the only person in the world to have spent more time on retirement calculators than me! This was Stuart Matthews of Pralana Consulting. He had been hard at work on the financial simulation technology that has grown into the PRC product line. The latest versions of his flagship offering, PRC/Gold, are in competition for the most powerful personal financial planning software on the planet.

The PRC calculators, created using Microsoft Excel, will run on either Windows or Mac platforms. The user interfaces are efficient and functional, but don't have the polish or snap of the latest web and desktop software. The products will be appealing to more technical users. However, PRC/Bronze, available via free download, is very easy to use. It offers three simple input screens, and generates long-term results that closely match those of PRC/Gold.

PRC/Silver, available at minimal cost, is like PRC/Bronze but adds support for three scenarios and lightweight sensitivity analysis. It allows the user to specify best, nominal, and worst settings for inflation and investment rates of return, and then presents those projections as an envelope of possible outcomes on an output graph. This is an alternative to more sophisticated Monte Carlo and historical analysis, and is more easily understandable by most people.

PRC/Gold is by far the most powerful tool in the Pralana lineup. It performs detailed federal income and

FICA tax calculations. It features all three mechanisms for modeling returns, and offers an area graph that integrates those fixed rate, Monte Carlo, and historical analyses to illustrate the upper and lower ranges of likely outcomes.

It offers very flexible input for your assets. You can set the average rate of return, standard deviation, and investment expenses for each asset class. You can set an asset allocation for each type of account (regular, tax-deferred, and Roth). You can also describe income streams in great detail, with control over pre-retirement, self-employment, pension, post-retirement, alimony, child support, windfalls (stock options, inheritance), and a fixed annuity. The program calculates your actual Social Security benefit based on your start age, handles spousal and survivor benefits, and can optimize your claiming decision.

PRC/Gold includes extensive capabilities for modeling the disposition of your property. You can set up scenarios for downsizing a home, or managing rental properties, and model changing ownership costs such as interest, taxes, insurance, and maintenance. It offers extensive support for discretionary expenses at different phases of life: pre-retirement, early post-retirement, late post-retirement, as well as after the death of the retiree or spouse. There are also optional withdrawal strategies applicable to discretionary spending. Much attention has gone into the modeling of *health care* expenses: You can set a separate inflation rate for health care. And you can also model those expenses for different phases of life: working, retirement for one or both of you, on Medicare, and after one spouse has died.

PRC/Gold's output is rich in both graphical and tabular formats. You can easily compare multiple scenarios. It also offers sensitivity evaluation that lets you dial various critical parameters up or down, and observe the impact on your future assets.

PRC/Gold is a clear leader, but, with other solid choices above at different price and feature levels, plus the many retirement calculators reviewed on my blog, you should have no trouble finding several good tools to analyze your retirement situation.

Take Action

- Evaluate and choose at least *two* retirement calculators to develop a picture or "model" of your assets and cash flow leading up to and during retirement. (If you have a preferred retirement calculator or a trusted financial institution already, start there. Then consult the reviews of calculators here and at *CanIRetireYet.com* for other choices.)

- When the calculator requires you to enter inflation rates or investment returns, start with the historical averages, but make them a little more conservative, by 1% to 2%. (Just realize that every assumption compounds the potential error in your answer.)

- If the calculator doesn't perform detailed tax calculations, thus requiring you to enter an *effective tax rate*, choose the value carefully. Use a free tool like the *TurboTax TaxCaster* to estimate a realistic tax rate for your retirement. It will likely be far lower than when you were working.

- When you must enter a life expectancy, base it on your family history, the Life Expectancy tables in *IRS Publication 590-B*, or the web sites LivingTo100.com or BlueZones.com – which will try to predict your longevity based on the latest research.

- Re-analyze your situation at least twice a year as you approach retirement. Try different scenarios, so you get a feel for the impact of potential changes to key retirement variables. This is much more useful and realistic than concentrating on a single, simplistic retirement "number."

- Share the output of your analysis in easily understood graphs or tables with your spouse, if you have one, so they too can develop a feel for your financial trajectory.

4: ANALYZING THE FUTURE

*"Planning for the future is like going fishing in a dry gulch;
Nothing ever works out as you wanted, so give up all your
schemes and ambitions."* — Gyalse Rinpoche

*"...face up to two unpleasant facts: The future is never
clear, and you pay a very high price...for a cheery
consensus."* — Warren Buffett

If you retire with some investments, minimal pension, and
Social Security, how do you live off your savings? How do
you know what you can spend each year without running
out, given that you don't know future investment returns,
inflation, or how long you will live? It's a thorny problem.

Simplistic answers such as "spend the average return on
your portfolio" were disproven by the mid 1990's. The first
phase of research into safe withdrawal rates produced the
"4% Rule" which stood for more than a decade. It says that
you can live on about 4% of your initial portfolio, adjusted
for inflation annually, without fear of running out over a 30-
year retirement. But new studies are seriously questioning
that simple rule. And real-world retirees know that living on
a fixed amount each year isn't realistic.

In this section we dig into the details of your retirement
projection. We compute some actual retirement scenarios to
understand the source of uncertainty in retirement
calculations. Then we review some tips and techniques for
more accurate calculations.

Next we look at what researchers past and present can tell us about our financial futures. What exactly is a "safe" withdrawal rate, and is it a constant value over time? What is the range of possibilities for safe withdrawals according to the latest studies? Given that range, how much savings might *you* actually need in retirement?

Finally, what does your personal expense and asset profile tell you about your probable retirement journey? Will you be walking, driving, or cruising through retirement? When we're done with this section, you should have the most realistic assessment yet of your retirement prospects.

Uncertainty in Retirement Calculations

Remember the game of *Telephone*? Players whisper a secret message down the line from one person to the next. When the message reaches the end of the line, it's repeated aloud to the group. And, without fail, it's been mangled beyond recognition!

Retirement planning can be like that. Seemingly small differences in input can compound into gigantic differences in output.

It's a serious problem, both in retirement and planning for it. In many cases, the range of input to your retirement equation creates an uncertainty interval so wide that it makes predicting the future absurd.

In this post, we'll look at a simple scenario that demonstrates the problem: I'll show how much the uncertainty in key variables such as growth rate, inflation rate, and life span can impact your ending net worth. Then, we'll discuss solutions.

Best Case/Worst Case

To better understand uncertainty in retirement calculations, I tested a simple retirement scenario: a couple retiring at age 60 with initial retirement savings of $500K and annual expenses of $40K. They start taking the average Social Security benefit at age 65, and they pay an overall effective tax rate in retirement of 5%. Let's see what happens to them under different conditions....

Earlier we reviewed the three unknowns that dominate retirement calculations. Let's start with those three variables, and add a few others. Altogether, we'll consider the best and worst cases for *five* input parameters to the retirement equation:

Investment returns — Given low interest rates and high stock market valuations, most experts are predicting reduced investment returns going forward. But within that dim outlook there is plenty of variation. In a recent 30-year market forecast, Rick Ferri called for U.S. large-cap stocks to return 5.0% before inflation, and 10-year investment-grade corporate bonds to return 2.6%. In a 50/50 portfolio that would be a **3.8%** real rate of return. Let's call that our best case. In a post last year Allan Roth drew from William Bernstein's *Rational Expectations* and from Robert Arnott to come up with a **1.5%** real rate of return for a 50/50 portfolio. Let's call that our worst case.

Inflation — While it's trendy now to fret about inflation, it's been relatively tame for decades. If you look at the historical record for inflation you can spot double-digit inflation in the past, but it's never lasted long. For our simulation let's assume the "best case" for inflation is **2.0%** – about 1.0% below the long-term average. And let's assume the worst case is **4.0%** – 1.0% above that average. Sure, inflation could spike. But, as you'll shortly see, even at 1% above the average, it does plenty of damage....

Life expectancy — Nobody knows how long they'll live. But we each have family history to draw on. Also, we know that modern health care is steadily improving. For our purposes here, let's use some mainstream numbers from the Social Security Administration: "A man reaching age 65 today can expect to live, on average, until age 84.3." and "About one out of every four 65-year-olds today will live past age 90, and one out of 10 will live past age 95." So let's call age **84** our best case (financially speaking), and age **95** our worst case. (The longer you live, the more chance you'll run out of money, so that's a worst case for financial planning.)

Social Security — Most of us will rely on Social Security to some extent. The average benefit in 2015 was about $1,335 per person for retired workers. But we've seen that Social Security is threatened and could be subject to cutbacks. Let's say the best case is that our hypothetical couple will receive their $1,335/month x 12 months x 2 people, or about **$32K** annually in benefits. And let's say the worst case is that they'll only receive about 75% of that, or about **$24K** annually.

Expenses — Budgets are personal, but for purposes of our simulation let's say our frugal couple needs to get by on about $40K/year. But living expenses aren't static. They'll vary with life events and with the economy. Personally, we spend more than this model couple. And still we've seen unsettling fluctuations in our retirement budget already. Some of it has been discretionary fun, but health care expenses have been particularly alarming. We've already seen 25% deviations from our retirement budget in a single year. So, while our couple's best case expenses may be $40K/year, let's say their worst case is another 25%, or $50K/year.

Sensitivity Analysis

So that's the input for our scenario. Nothing too far-fetched here. The best cases don't sound wildly optimistic. The worst cases don't sound particularly dire. Each number is entirely feasible, within a range supported by the data and the experts. But what happens when we put these numbers all together in one simulation?

The results are surprising. Let's start with the best-case scenario and proceed gradually to the worst....

The best-case scenario involves low inflation, high investment returns, full Social Security, no changes in living expenses, and shorter lifespan. Under those conditions, our couple reaches the end of their lives at 84 and leaves a nice $477K for their beneficiaries. If they are fortunate enough to live longer, their net worth keeps growing: At age 95 it would be **$587K**.

(Note these numbers and those that follow are adjusted to today's dollars, for ease of comparison.)

Now let's introduce our first worst-case scenario. What if inflation runs at 4.0%? We crunch the numbers again. Now the net worth at age 95 is about **$568K** in today's dollars. The impact of inflation is muted because most of our couple's cash flow is inflation-adjusted in some form.

What next? How about if real investment returns are reduced to 1.5%? Well, now their ending net worth at age 95 is only **$143K**.

Then what if they are only able to collect 75% of their Social Security? Now their net worth drops into negative

territory at age 95, to **-$167K**, implying they ran out of
money years before.

Now what if their expenses increase by a real 25% on top of
all the other bad news? This really hurts. Their net worth
now plummets to **-$647K** at age 95, implying an even
earlier end to their retirement funds. (To have stayed afloat
at their current lifestyle to age 95, they'd need to have
raised an extra $647K.)

Reviewing each year in this final scenario, with all of these
worst case factors compounded, we see that at age 75 – just
15 years after retiring – our unfortunate couple is *broke*.

What's the takeaway? In bracketing the key input variables
to the retirement equation by modest, realistic amounts,
we've seen *dramatic* differences in retirement outcomes
years later. In fact, the difference in ending net worth
between our best- and worst-case scenarios at age 95 is well
more than *one million dollars*.

Here is how the different variables contribute to that gap
between the scenarios:

increased inflation	1.5%
decreased investment returns	34.4%
reduced Social Security	25.1%
increased living expenses	38.9%

Investment returns, which get so much attention here and
elsewhere, are critical to this particular couple's retirement
trajectory. Most of the difference between the best- and
worst-case scenarios is accounted for by investment returns,

Social Security, and living expenses. And it's sobering to realize that we have little individual control over the first two of those factors. While the last one, expenses, we control only partially, until it comes to health care or emergencies.

Keeping Perspective
Before panicking, remember this scenario isn't *your* retirement. And, though I wasn't using outlandish numbers, this is still an analysis of "extremes." That's because it's unlikely that all variables would be at their worst or best values simultaneously.

But it isn't impossible: Ever had more than one thing go wrong at once? How about two or three? It happens more frequently than we'd like, and that's when serious problems begin.

In analyzing these extremes, we are looking at the *envelope* of retirement possibilities. Using a *Monte Carlo* simulation, with output in percentiles, would communicate the *interior* of that envelope better than I'm attempting here. But, I lean to simplicity – looking at the best, worst, and average cases. Just know that focusing only on the extremes, or the averages, could be deceiving. There is also value in pondering the probabilities of the interior.

The range in results for this simple simulation drives home that retirement modeling is better at studying and comparing *different options*, than it is at producing absolute *answers*: What if my child goes to a private college versus the state school? What happens if I downsize my family house versus retiring in place? What are the tax implications if I convert my Traditional IRA into a Roth? None of these scenarios requires an absolutely correct numerical answer, as long as the alternatives can be compared reliably.

When it comes to absolute answers to the big questions, "When can I retire?" or "How much money will I leave behind?", retirement calculators simply cannot reliably predict your *endpoint*. They can only give your *direction*. A retirement model is a **compass**, not a **map**. It can tell you where you're going, but not if and when you'll arrive!

Eliminating Variables

Don't like those uncertainties? Then you can try eliminating some of the variables:

- If you don't like the uncertainty and volatility of the stock market, you can annuitize some of your assets.

- If you're concerned about inflation, you can add inflation riders to your annuities, or hold assets like inflation-protected bonds, commodities, real estate, or more stocks.

- If you can't get a handle on life expectancy then, in addition to loading up on annuities, you can use an infinite time horizon for your planning – living off dividends and growth without touching principal. This approach is especially wise if you retire early and expect to live a long time.

- If you're going to rely on Social Security and don't trust the government to make good on its promises, then you can work longer to build other assets. This

> pays off in multiple ways: increasing your life savings and your eventual Social Security benefit, plus reducing the time you will rely on it.

Ultimately, the retirement decision is less about your *number* and more about your quality of life going forward. The range of possible outcomes is huge. And no matter how many numbers you throw at the decision, you or an advisor will ultimately be making a gut determination based on numerical probabilities, personal values, and what you want out of life.

Tips for More Accurate Retirement Calculations

As we've just seen, even the most careful retirement calculations can produce answers that vary by hundreds of percent. If we have this much difficulty achieving precision in a simplified, artificial scenario, what should we expect in our real-world retirements?

Fact is, coaxing realistic answers out of a retirement calculator takes knowledge and good judgment. Even with that, nobody can predict the future perfectly. But there are some steps anyone can follow to get more accurate results. These tips will help you stay out of the ditch, ensure results that are as good as possible, and improve your odds of getting useful guidance out of a retirement calculator:

1. Setting Social Security and Retirement Dates: In a traditional retirement, you quit working at 65 and begin taking Social Security. But we are no longer in a traditional working world. Retirement simply begins when you *stop working*: That could be early, if you're frugal and fortunate, or it could be much later. Social Security, on the other hand, begins sometime between ages 62 and 70 – depending on your financial situation and your strategy for taking benefits. Equating these two events – retirement and Social Security – is archaic and usually incorrect. Yet a surprising number of retirement calculators do it anyway. For the most accuracy, choose a higher-fidelity calculator that can handle these events separately.

2. Including a Spouse: Not all calculators can handle distinct financial data for a spouse: separate salaries, savings, and Social Security, for example. This is OK in some cases. It's often easy and accurate enough to combine your salaries and savings. But it can be a problem when dates are involved. If your spouse is retiring on a different schedule from you, collecting Social Security or a pension at different times, a calculator needs to handle the correct timing. Otherwise the results will be off, perhaps way off, especially if there is a large difference in your spouse's age or career path. To get serious about the fidelity of your retirement calculations, you'll need a calculator that tracks your spouse's finances separately.

3. Replacing Income vs. Tracking Expenses: A number of calculators insist on modeling your retirement living expenses as a percent of your pre-retirement income. While this is OK as a very rough estimate in your accumulation stage, it doesn't cut it for those nearing or in retirement, especially early retirement. In the latter cases, you don't even *have* an income. Some calculators adapt, and others simply can't handle these situations. Fact is, income and expenses are not necessarily related for many people, especially diligent savers and early retirees. The best way for you to know your expenses is to actually track them yourself. The best way for a calculator to know your expenses is for you to enter them explicitly. If your lifestyle is unique in any way, then the one-size-fits-all or income-based expense estimates used by some lower-fidelity calculators are likely to be wildly inaccurate.

4. Making Inflation Assumptions: Many calculators incorporate a built-in rate of inflation, usually somewhere in the range of 2.5% to 4.0%. But some calculators don't document their inflation assumption for users. You need to know. Because your point of view could be different. You might think that inflation will match the historical average going forward, or that it will be somewhat or much higher. Either way, a retirement calculator is setting itself up for obsolescence by fixing that inflation value, and not letting you change it. For a complete picture, you should be able to vary the rate of inflation, and investigate alternative scenarios as part of your retirement analysis.

5. Inflating vs. Reducing Spending as You Age: The typical retirement calculator automatically and mindlessly increases your retirement expenses every year by your specified rate of inflation. That sounds reasonable, at first glance. Yet my experience and that of other retirees demonstrate that your personal rate of inflation is only distantly related to the government's official inflation rate. Research shows that most people's expenses decline as they age. Even with higher health care expenses, you simply aren't able to consume as much at 80 as you did at 60. Though your lifestyle could always be an outlier, in reality, most retirees are going to see a reduction in their living expenses over the years. The best calculators can account for this, or at least give you options to model it.

6. Choosing Investment Returns: More perhaps than for any other parameter, you need flexibility in setting stock and bond market investment returns. Nobody knows what these are going to be in the future. Many experts feel that even historical averages going back 100 years or more are not a sound guideline. Helping you understand the range of return possibilities should be one of the primary functions of a good retirement calculator. And it's best if a calculator can offer you a diversity of opinions. You don't want to put all your money on one horse. Ideally, you should be able to run simulations using each of the three main approaches for modeling returns: average, historical, and Monte Carlo. Then, be able to compare the results. Even within each of these algorithms, you'll want to vary inputs. When using average returns, for example, do it using both the optimistic long-term historical averages, plus the more pessimistic numbers suggested by experts based on current market conditions.

7. Including Investment Expenses: If you are a low-cost, passive index investor enjoying razor-thin expense ratios on your portfolio in the sub 0.2% range, you might get away with ignoring investment expenses in your calculations. But if you employ a financial advisor, trade positions often, or use actively managed funds, you'd better account for investment expenses. They can consume a truly astounding portion of your wealth over the long haul. In one real-world simulation I performed that incorporated a 1.4% expense ratio over 30 years, the financial manager walked away with nearly 25% of the investor's hard-earned money over time! Lesson learned: high expenses matter. Ignore them at your own peril. And, if a calculator doesn't offer specific input fields for tracking investment expenses, then you'll need to subtract them before entering market returns.

8. Selecting Tax Rates: Though tax rates have not been critical in my middle-income, early retirement, taxes are still important. And, the higher your income, the more important they become. Even for those who expect a modest lifestyle in retirement, substantially higher income during the working years requires special consideration. That's why, if you're still working, a calculator needs to offer both pre- and post- retirement tax rates. Also, calculators need to distinguish carefully between *effective* and *marginal* rates. Your effective tax rate is your total tax paid divided by *all* of your income. Your marginal rate is the amount of tax you pay on your last dollar of income. That is a function of your tax bracket, and is nearly always much higher than your effective rate. The vast majority of calculators use an effective rate, but many don't document or explain that fact very well. And you won't know your effective rate unless you, or your tax software, compute it based on your tax return and realistic retirement projections. If you mistakenly enter a marginal rate into a retirement calculator, you will grossly overestimate your tax liability!

9. Withdrawing Among Multiple Accounts: If you're concerned about taxes in retirement, then you also need a retirement calculator that can manage your wealth in multiple accounts corresponding to the three possible tax treatments: taxable, tax-free, and tax-deferred. (Higher-fidelity calculators will offer conventional brokerage accounts, Roth IRAs, and Traditional IRAs.) Each of these accounts has different tax consequences as money flows in, grows over time, and flows out. If a calculator offers anything less than these three types of accounts, it won't be able to accurately model your tax liability over the years. A good calculator will model each type of account correctly, and will also help you optimize the sequence of your retirement withdrawals, to minimize your taxes.

10. Working in Retirement: Calculators that assume a traditional retirement scenario where you quit working at age 65, take Social Security right away, then head out to play golf for the rest of your days, simply can't handle modern retirements. For starters, whether by choice or not, many of us retire from our main careers earlier. And then many of us work part-time in new, "encore" careers. So, often we *do* have some work-related income in retirement. For some of us, that's an essential part of the plan. For others it's an unintended side effect of a favorite hobby. Either way, a calculator that can't handle some notion of post-retirement "work" is just plain out-of-step with reality. Without the ability to account for post-retirement income, a calculator will have you working longer at your main career, limiting your options for maximizing life.

For all their sophistication, retirement calculators still face an impossible job – predicting the future. To get the best picture or model of your retirement, use the information in this book to choose the best retirement calculator for you. Then apply the ten tips above to make sure the answers it computes are as accurate as possible.

"Safe" Withdrawal Rates

Retirement calculators attempt to give you a detailed picture of the actual cash flow throughout your retirement. They try to model future reality so you can draw conclusions about how to run your specific financial life. But, for the last few decades, various academic researchers have been running similar, generic simulations, and using them to derive various simple rules of thumb for retirement income. The starting point for these rules is the notion of a "safe" withdrawal rate.

How do we know the expected lifetime of an investment portfolio when some portion of it is consumed month after month, year after year? The truth is that we don't. Nobody does. Even insurance companies that sell annuity contracts for a lump sum, promising you a monthly payment for the rest of your life, can't fundamentally guarantee that income stream. All that exists to back up their promise are odds and statistics and the cash flow of the company. And, when managed carefully and conservatively, and backed up by fiscally responsible reinsurers and governments, that's probably a reasonable bet.

So odds and statistics are all we've got. But we've got a lot of those. Countless studies and projections over the years have established a range for the safe withdrawal rate – the amount of money you can withdraw from a well-diversified portfolio each year and expect it to last for a lengthy retirement.

The bad news is that this safe withdrawal rate is significantly less than the average historical return on your particular mix of investments.

You can't simply consume all your income or growth in good years. Why? Because your real-world investments won't perform the average each year, and they may *underperform* at the start of your retirement, thereby damaging your principal's ability to produce income for you later on. We've already touched on this phenomenon, known as "sequence of returns" risk.

A safe withdrawal rate sounds like a simple concept, but there are some common misconceptions:

For starters, safe withdrawal rates are designed to be *independent* of your investment returns in any one year. In other words, you don't have to worry about how your investments are performing at any given time, as long as you withdraw no more than the "safe" rate. These rates take into account historical growth, and losses, on typical balanced portfolios of stocks and bonds, to specify a withdrawal amount that won't deplete your portfolio over the course of a typical retirement.

Another common confusion about safe withdrawal rates is whether they mean a certain *percentage* or a *fixed amount* is to be withdrawn from your portfolio each year. In fact, the traditional studies specify a *fixed amount* beginning at some percentage of the initial portfolio, adjusted annually for inflation, to be withdrawn each year. Mathematically speaking, that's quite different from withdrawing a fixed *percentage* of portfolio value each year. It's important to understand that, withdrawing a fixed amount adjusted for inflation, your lifestyle doesn't fluctuate. And it is entirely possible to completely *deplete* your portfolio, at which time your lifestyle suffers a complete collapse. On the other hand, withdrawing a certain *percentage* or proportion each year will *never* deplete a portfolio, though your income could fluctuate substantially over time – and so your lifestyle is not guaranteed.

The Rise and Fall of the 4% Rule

"How much money do you need to retire?" Amazingly, there was little research aimed at answering this question until about the mid-1990's. Some of the first answers were shown to be overly simplistic, but for a decade or so we enjoyed relative consensus around the easily understood **4% Rule**. That rule says, in essence, that you must save about 25 times your annual expenses, or that you can withdraw about 4% of your portfolio in the first year of retirement and then adjust that amount for inflation each year, with little chance of running out over a 30-year retirement.

But the era of the simple 4% Rule is drawing to a close. We are now hearing from respected voices that it is rigid and simplistic – relying too much on historical data, and not enough on current financial conditions. Most alarmingly, we are being told that it might be too generous for extreme economic times, that the actual safe withdrawal rate for today's retirees could be as low as *half* the traditional 4% rate.

It's a shocking development, and one that we all need to take seriously. But, before we consider the possible impact on us, and look at actions we can take to cope, let's review how we got to this point. Understanding the various approaches to figuring safe withdrawal rates will eliminate some misconceptions at the outset and put the venerable 4% Rule in context:

Toward a Safe Withdrawal Rate

The Layman's Method — We've all heard that stocks have delivered total returns, on average, of approximately 10% annually over the last century. The obvious conclusion by an uninformed layman would be that you can consume 10% of your portfolio in retirement each year. For example, you might spend $50,000 annually from a half-million-dollar portfolio. This was actually the conventional thinking when I first started looking at early retirement about 20 years ago. Unfortunately, it is dead wrong, for a number of reasons. For starters, it doesn't take inflation into account.

Considering Inflation — When we say the long-term return for stocks has averaged 10%, we must not forget that a portion of that "growth" is actually inflation in the unit of measurement – the dollar itself. The long-term inflation rate in the U.S. has been in the neighborhood of 3%. (I'm rounding all numbers for simplicity.) So the actual growth in the stock market has been more like 10% - 3% = 7% in real (inflation-adjusted) terms. Thus, for the purposes of withdrawing a sum with constant purchasing power in retirement, we can only use 7% of our portfolio in the first year, if we are to account for the fact that our *expenses* will be growing with inflation too. So now our retirement purchasing power is down to 7% of our portfolio. Unfortunately, this number is still dead wrong, because it doesn't take into account the possibility that bad things could happen in the stock market at the start of our retirement.

Insuring Against Sequence of Returns Risk — The two previously described, simple-minded analyses make a fatal assumption – that stock market returns will be "average" each year. But that just isn't so. For example, in a recent four-year stretch, the Dow Jones Industrial Average delivered one year of single-digit returns, two years of double-digit returns, and one year of *negative* double-digit returns. Anything but average, or consistent! So what happens if you experience some of those negative returns in the first decade of your retirement? We won't go into a detailed mathematical analysis here, but it's not too hard to imagine that your portfolio would be damaged and might be unable to provide for you in the future. This is *sequence of returns* risk. And insuring against it requires lopping a few more percentage points off the safe withdrawal rate. In *The Four Pillars of Investing*, market wizard William Bernstein writes that you pay a penalty of about 1.5% to 2% for "luck of the draw."

Birth of the 4% Rule

The first person to quantify this required insurance was William Bengen, in 1994. He searched for "the highest sustainable withdrawal rate for the worst-case retirement scenario" in history. He used historical data over rolling 30-year periods, and found that, for a 50/50 allocation to stocks and bonds, the value was 4.15%. *This was the start of the 4% Rule.*

In 1998, an article appeared by three Trinity University professors of finance, since dubbed the "Trinity Study." The professors chose a different bond index for their balanced portfolio. But their findings were essentially the same: Portfolios of at least 50% stocks had 95% or higher success rates for periods up to 30 years when using a 4% withdrawal rate, adjusted for inflation.

Subsequent studies by a number of individuals and institutions – using both historical returns and Monte Carlo simulations featuring random inputs – have confirmed a range centered on that 4% withdrawal rate. Thus began the simple and seemingly sound 4% Rule, which has been mainstream retirement planning advice for more than a decade....

Warning Signs

Also published in 1998 was a seemingly unrelated paper on investing returns that has become the basis for *undermining* the 4% Rule nearly 15 years later.

John Campbell and Robert Shiller found that certain stock market metrics, particularly P/E 10 (price divided by average real earnings for the previous 10 years), are useful in forecasting future stock price changes. A version of that ratio known as CAPE (Cyclically Adjusted Price-to-Earnings) is said to be especially accurate, because there is such a long series of data available, and because it's based on professional evaluations of businesses, not predictions about the future.

The conclusion of Campbell and Shiller's analysis was that we must expect substantial declines in real stock returns when the market has reached high valuations. But, what does their work on valuations have to do with the 4% Rule?

Well, another researcher, Wade Pfau, recently used Campbell and Shiller's technique and connected sustainable withdrawal rates to market valuation levels on the date of retirement. He showed that sustainable withdrawal rates for portfolios *going forward* were highly correlated to the level of the stock market at the *time of retirement*!

To quote Pfau, "*...the news for recent retirees is not good.*" The 4% withdrawal rate simply isn't safe when stock market valuations are at historical highs and yields are at historical lows. Unfortunately, his model predicts that sustainable withdrawal rates have fallen **below 2%** since 2003! And, if that's not news enough, Pfau has initiated other research showing that high safe withdrawal rates in the U.S. might be a historical anomaly compared to the rest of the world.

Pfau's conclusions are a potential bombshell for retirement planning. He's essentially saying that modern retirements could be *twice* as expensive as we had planned!

What are we to make of this? The research is relatively new and still open to debate. To some extent we are in uncharted terrain: It may or may not be correct to extrapolate from the past. It's usually wise to prepare for the worst. But, fact is, I've now been retired for *half a decade*, based on planning originally around the 4% Rule, and my portfolio has not behaved particularly poorly in retirement. We're better off now than when we started.

Traditionally, there have been two applications for the 4% Rule. The first is in asking the question, "How much do I need to retire?" The 4% Rule produced the common rule of thumb that you should save 25 times your annual expenses. I still think that is a good guideline for a retirement nest egg, *IF it is not the only thing between you and destitution.* That is, if you can count on some baseline of Social Security, pension, or annuity, and you are retiring at an age when you have options for returning to work, or part-time work. Those resources give you choices for optimizing your future finances. So, in my opinion, the simple 4% Rule is still a reasonable metric for those with flexibility....

The second application of the 4% Rule has been in actually living off your assets *after* you have retired. Here I think the old rule is, in fact, obsolete, and may have been obsolete for some time. It is far too static, and, as we have seen, possibly unsafe. Followed blindly in today's market conditions, it could wipe out your portfolio long before the end of your life. Fortunately, most retirees instinctively reduce expenses when times are hard, and today that instinct is more important than ever.

The ultimate answer lies in the usual three strategies for financial success: saving more, spending less, and optimizing how we manage our money. And, when it comes to withdrawing from a portfolio to fund a multi-decade retirement, I think that the last point – optimizing money management – holds particular promise.

The ultimate answer, I believe, for coping with the demise of the 4% Rule, is in *dynamically navigating your retirement years*. Your lifestyle must be calibrated to economic realities and may need to *change* as you make your way through retirement. And that is the subject of section 5 of this book, where we discuss strategies for dynamically living off your assets in retirement.

Bracketing the Possible

Now that we've dug into some of the history and research around safe withdrawal rates, we can step back for the big picture.

There have been hundreds of studies into how much you need to retire, and nearly as many systems proposed for how to safely spend down your assets in retirement. In essence, these efforts break down into three categories:

"Backcasting" using market history: These approaches use historical data about markets and economies over the last hundred years, plus or minus. They run your personal numbers through every possible set of conditions experienced in the past, under the theory that things probably won't be worse, or better, than they have been. Bengen and the Trinity Study were the originators of this approach, and it lives on in many modern retirement calculators.

Forecasting using history, or current market valuations: Some of these approaches use historical averages plus standard deviations in Monte Carlo simulations in an attempt to map the envelope of future possibilities. Other approaches, like Pfau's, note that there have been strong correlations in the past between market valuations and future performance. So they use *current* market valuations to predict how assets might fare in the future. All of these approaches assume, in their own way, that past behavior will be replicated into the future, and that no fundamental paradigm shifts have occurred that would change how assets are valued.

Making like an endowment: These approaches treat your assets like an endowment, intended to last indefinitely. They attempt to consume only the inflation-adjusted income and growth. In their simplest incarnation they might dictate living off stock dividends, or interest from bond or CD ladders. They could consume all available income, or some designated fixed percentage of assets each year. The traditional payout rate for many long-standing endowments and charitable trusts is **5%**. Annuities offer a similar mechanism, with payout rates in the 5% to 6% range for couples in their 60's, as I write this.

In the end, every one of these approaches boils down to this: A certain *percentage* of your assets is deemed safe to consume at the start of retirement. Sometimes that initial percentage is adjusted for inflation in following years, so the nominal amount withdrawn increases over time. Sometimes the percentage itself is maintained, so the amount withdrawn fluctuates and is proportional to the size of the underlying portfolio. Either way, each of these approaches settles on an initial withdrawal percentage.

And, after the better part of a decade studying and reading about this question, I can tell you that essentially all methods arrive at the same range of initial payout rates from your assets: between **2%** on the very low side for the most conservative approaches, and **6%** on the very high side, for the most optimistic approaches. Almost no responsible party currently recommends a withdrawal rate over 5% at the start of retirement. More and more are recommending lower rates – as low as 2% to 3%, given the state of world financial affairs, and unknown prospects for future growth.

If we throw out the outliers, we can say that the consensus view on this issue is **3%** to **5%**. Large endowments, respected financial companies, leading researchers, well-known financial advisors, best-selling authors, and successful early-retired bloggers all generally advise withdrawal rates within that range.

I could stake my own specific claim in this debate, trying to dictate a precise initial withdrawal rate in retirement. But it would be pointless. I am 99% confident that the correct answer can be found within that 3-5% range, and that no more precise answer is possible. *Because, again, this is an attempt to predict an unknown future.*

So there you have it. If you want to be *absolutely certain* that you don't run out of money over the course of a lengthy retirement, you'd better consume less than 3% of your assets annually at the start. If you have some lifestyle flexibility, 3% to 4% looks pretty safe to me. Later in retirement, or with a strong economic tailwind at the start, you might get away with 4% to 5%.

In my opinion, this is the most useful and accurate statement that can be made on the matter.

How Much Do You Need?

So we have explored your retirement expenses and income, the present value of your pensions and Social Security, and the range of possible safe withdrawal rates. We now know enough for a rough assessment of your required retirement savings.

The table below gives you a target savings number based on your lifestyle (required monthly income) and your expectations for the future (safe withdrawal rate). If you can live frugally, pick a lower income. If you need a more luxurious retirement, choose a higher income. If you're pessimistic about the future, pick a lower withdrawal rate. If you're more optimistic, or have the flexibility to adapt to events, pick a higher withdrawal rate.

There are two possible and equally simple approaches to using this table:

1. You can work with your total living expenses in the first column, and count the present value of any pensions and Social Security against the retirement savings number you find in subsequent columns.
2. Or, you can think in terms of your income shortfall. To find that, you subtract your guaranteed income such as pensions, Social Security, and annuities from your living expenses, and look up the resulting number in the first column. (But then you would not add the present value of your other income streams to the required savings.)

Table: Required Retirement Savings

Required Monthly Income	Savings for 3% Withdrawal	Savings for 4% Withdrawal	Savings for 5% Withdrawal
$2,000	$800,000	$600,000	$480,000
$2,500	$1,000,000	$750,000	$600,000
$3,000	$1,200,000	$900,000	$720,000
$3,500	$1,400,000	$1,050,000	$840,000
$4,000	$1,600,000	$1,200,000	$960,000
$4,500	$1,800,000	$1,350,000	$1,080,000
$5,000	$2,000,000	$1,500,000	$1,200,000
$5,500	$2,200,000	$1,650,000	$1,320,000
$6,000	$2,400,000	$1,800,000	$1,440,000
$6,500	$2,600,000	$1,950,000	$1,560,000
$7,000	$2,800,000	$2,100,000	$1,680,000
$7,500	$3,000,000	$2,250,000	$1,800,000
$8,000	$3,200,000	$2,400,000	$1,920,000
$8,500	$3,400,000	$2,550,000	$2,040,000
$9,000	$3,600,000	$2,700,000	$2,160,000

A secure retirement requires considerable assets. In many cases, you do need $1 million or more in savings to retire comfortably. Though Social Security, a frugal lifestyle, and a part-time retirement gig can all work to reduce that number.

That's it. Simple assumptions, simple calculations, simple answer. In my opinion this is all the accuracy that's needed or possible at the start of a long retirement. More important than a faux-accurate retirement "number" is understanding how your finances fit into the envelope of possibilities, preparing adequately for the journey, and navigating wisely whatever economic conditions arise during your retirement years....

Your Retirement Journey: Walking, Driving, or Cruising?

We've dissected the retirement equation, and seen it in action. We've settled on a consensus band of initial payout rates between 3% and 5%. There is little precedent for withdrawal rates outside of that range for a lengthy retirement. Most likely you would wind up with far too much, or too little, money.

So, what is your personal situation? Given your current or projected savings, will you be *walking*, *driving*, or *cruising* through retirement? Let's answer that question now: Divide your expected annual retirement living expenses by your savings at retirement and find your initial withdrawal rate.

First the good news, for the well-off: If your rate is less than about 2% to 3%, you will almost surely be *cruising* through retirement. Short of "black swan" events, there is no historical precedent for you to have money worries in retirement. You should be able to make it through your golden years without concern for economic conditions. Just note, this is no license for carelessness: Your investments still need to be managed intelligently, and your costs need to be kept under that 2% to 3% threshold.

Next the news that applies to many of us: If your withdrawal rate falls *within* that proven envelope, about 3-5%, then you have the opportunity of *driving* yourself through retirement. You can make it, but not without a keen eye on your finances. Not only must your investments be intelligently managed, and must you keep your costs within the prescribed range, but you may have to *adjust your lifestyle* based on economic conditions. This is particularly true in the critical first decade of retirement, when you cannot afford to damage your portfolio. If there is an extended recession, or a period of low growth or punishing inflation, you will have to react in order to keep your withdrawal rate in the safe range. You would need to generate some additional income, if able, or cut expenses if not. On the other hand, if times are good, or even just *normal*, you can enjoy some splurges in your retirement lifestyle, and may even grow your portfolio and leave a financial legacy.

Last the bad news, for those who haven't saved enough: If your initial withdrawal rate is greater than about 5%, odds are strongly against your assets lasting through a lengthy retirement. You are unfortunately going to be *walking* through retirement, and your lifestyle is at risk for serious disruption. If you can take action soon enough to significantly increase your income or reduce your expenses, then you may still be able to provide for retirement living essentials while avoiding the worst-case scenarios. But, otherwise, hardship looms in later years, with nothing but Social Security or other minimal social welfare programs as a safety net.

I sincerely hope you are in one of the first two groups, or can be. The rest of this book will be focused on those of us living in that 3% to 5% range for retirement, the middle group. Because these are the people who both *need* help, and *can* be helped. The upcoming final section of the book will address the strategies for those who are *driving* their retirements. We'll discuss the tools and techniques available to navigate that self-directed retirement journey, and what to do if threatening conditions develop, so you don't run off the road....

Take Action

- Refine your retirement plan using the tips for more accurate retirement calculations at the start of this section.
- Understand why you can't withdraw the average stock market return from your portfolio and expect it to survive. Understand the impact of inflation and sequence of returns risk on withdrawal rates.
- Learn about the safe withdrawal rate concept and understand the difference between a fixed withdrawal *amount* that is adjusted for inflation, versus a fixed withdrawal *percentage* that results in a variable amount to be withdrawn each year. (Neither is "right" or "wrong," but they will result in different retirement spending patterns.)
- Appreciate the difference between using a safe withdrawal rate, like the 4% Rule, to determine *how much* retirement savings you need, which can be reasonable, depending on your situation, versus actually *living off* your assets using a static rule, which is hopelessly inflexible in the face of future events.
- Review the bracket of possibilities for safe withdrawal rates – the highest and lowest possible payout rates identified by the research. Choose your own envelope *within* that bracket – the highest and lowest possible rates for you, depending on your views of the future, and your own lifestyle flexibility in retirement. (My recommendation is 3% to 5%, but opinions differ.)

- Using that personal bracket, your expected retirement living expenses, and the preceding savings table, identify the *most* and *least* you might have to save for retirement.
- Identify whether you'll be *walking*, *driving*, or *cruising* through retirement, and how you feel about those different destinies. If you'll be walking, take measures *now* to improve matters. If you'll be driving or cruising, then, congratulations, you've arrived at the starting gate. It's up to you to decide when to begin the journey....

5: NAVIGATING YOUR JOURNEY

"Only the present is within our reach. To care for the present is to care for the future." — Thich Nhat Hanh

"Everyone has a plan till they get punched in the mouth." — Mike Tyson

The future is uncertain. The variables are numerous and unpredictable. Any scenario we can compute, or even imagine, will shortly be outdated by events. The most confounding variable of all may be *life expectancy*: The only truly accurate answer to the retirement equation comes when you leave this world: Did you run out of money, or not?

The old, *optimistic* answer for retirement income was the 4% Rule. The old *pessimistic* answer was to live off only interest and dividends without touching principal. But, the new *realistic* answer, in my opinion, is that you must be prepared to *dynamically* manage your assets over a long retirement.

In retirement, you are departing on a journey into uncharted terrain. You have a compass for direction, but only the sketchiest of maps. You need the confidence to travel through that unknown terrain without getting stuck, or lost, or running out of supplies. You need enough information while you travel to avoid heading in the wrong direction, or turning back when you're almost there. That's what this section of the book is about....

We'll start by assessing the economy and your investment portfolio at the starting point of your retirement. What are the key asset classes for retirement, and what are the risks? Next we'll explore a number of techniques for managing withdrawals from your nest egg. Which is best for you?

We'll go on to discuss the warning signs of financial trouble in retirement, including a "fuel gauge" that can tell if you're running low. And, in case that happens, we'll cover the critical "lifeboat strategies" – on both the expense and income sides – that can save your retirement.

When you finish this section of the book, you'll have in hand the essential money management tools for beginning your retirement journey.

Knowing Your Starting Point: Economic Cycles

In November of 1972 the Dow Jones Industrial Average closed at a little above 1,000 points. Then it went down, and stayed mostly down, for the next *ten years*. While the Dow sat still, life went on. Finally, late in 1982, after 10 years, the Dow crossed the 1,000-point threshold again, on its way to new highs.

Retirement was different in the 1970's. Pensions were the norm. But had you been living primarily off your investments, the decade would have seemed an eternity. And it would have devastated an unprepared portfolio.

If you are early in retirement, a lengthy bear market is your *worst-case scenario*. It exposes your assets to damage that can't be recovered in your lifetime. It's happened before, and it could happen again. How do you prepare?

Earlier in the book we sized up your retirement expenses and assessed your retirement income. Those are essential personal factors to understand as you begin your retirement journey. They are comparable to choosing a vehicle and understanding its gas mileage. But you also have to look out the window! You need to understand where you are, and what kind of terrain you'll be driving through. You can't stick with a single speed or direction for a real-world journey, and you can't for the retirement journey either.

In retirement, you'll need to tap into an investment portfolio for any expenses not covered by guaranteed income streams such as pensions, Social Security, or annuities. A few will enjoy or get by with only guaranteed income, but the rest must deal with this question: When and how do you liquidate assets?

Study after study has shown that it is impossible to accurately predict the stock market. Economic cycles play out every decade or so, but their exact timing is not predictable, and the variations from one cycle to the next are significant.

However, it is possible to know, roughly, which part of the economic cycle the market is currently in, and therefore how your assets are valued today. Metrics like Robert Shiller's Cyclically Adjusted Price-to-Earnings ratio (CAPE) give us an indication of stock *valuations*. We also have historical data telling us, on average, how *long* market or business cycles have lasted in the past. With this data, you can make informed guesses about how to structure and manage your retirement assets.

For our purposes, living off assets in retirement, that is good enough. With few exceptions, the markets, and especially whole economies, do not change overnight. They gradually transition from one phase to another. And, in retirement, it is rarely necessary or wise to make major financial decisions quickly.

Bear Markets

The one routine decision you cannot escape in retirement is this: Do I need cash? And, if so, where should it come from? And, how long might I have to rely on conservative cash and fixed income investments to outlast a bear market?

The answer depends on how *long* market cycles last, on average. The Schwab Center for Financial Research has compiled statistics on the <u>time to recovery of a market decline</u> for recent history. It shows that, for the eight market declines from 1966 to 2009, the average time it took the S&P 500 Index to recover to prior highs was a little over **3 years**.

But that's an average. In retirement, when rebuilding assets by returning to work may be impossible, we are also concerned about *worst cases*. How bad could a bear market get? Wade Pfau has studied worst-case market declines going back to the early 20th century. His data on <u>real stock market losses larger than 50%</u> shows the number of years it took for real stock market value to again exceed the level prior to major market drops. Whether looking at the U.S. or a GDP-weighted "world" portfolio across 20 countries, that average worst-case recovery was about **9 years**.

Finally, we have the National Bureau of Economic Research (NBER), the organization that officially delineates business cycles. The NBER measures the length of all U.S. business cycle expansions and contractions. On their web site, we can see a list of business cycles going back to the 1800's. Though business cycles are not identical to market cycles, the statistics are strongly related. The stock market reflects the business cycle, often in advance. The NBER data shows the average time from peak to peak in 33 business cycles from 1854 to 2009 was 56.4 months, or a little less than **5 years**.

Defensive Asset Allocation

These numbers neatly bracket the critical time spans for liquidating assets in retirement. If you want to reduce or eliminate the risk of being forced to sell stocks at a loss, then you need to allocate your more conservative investments accordingly. Specifically, you need to multiply the above time spans in years by your required annual retirement income, and stockpile that much in conservative assets like cash, bonds, and reliable rental or annuity income. These are the assets most likely to hold their value during an extended downturn.

Bottom line, to outlast a run-of-the-mill bear market, you should have *three* years of cash on hand. And for a worst-case recession/depression, you'd better have close to a *decade* worth of cash, plus other conservative investments you could rely on once cash runs out.

Choosing Asset Classes for Retirement

To prepare for and respond to the economic cycle, you will need to focus on the *asset classes* in your investment portfolio. In identifying the key asset classes for a retirement portfolio, what should be your guidelines? Here are my simple criteria:

- The asset class should behave uniquely in response to phases of the economic cycle: growth/recession, inflation/deflation.

- The asset class should be easy to buy or sell, without high transaction costs.

- The asset class should be inexpensive to hold, without high expenses or maintenance costs.

- The asset class should be transparent and not require special expertise to manage or value.

The first point above is what makes a certain set of assets an "asset class." They are fundamentally different from other kinds of investments, giving them individual risk/return characteristics. What do we mean by "fundamentally different"? Rick Ferri explains this best: "Stocks and bonds are different; one is ownership and the other is loan. U.S. stocks are different from international stocks in base currency and government policy. Real estate and commodities differ from common stocks in collateral structure."

The hallmark of different asset classes is that they are "uncorrelated." For example, on a scale of -1.0 to +1.0

(negatively correlated to positively correlated), the correlation between the U.S. stock market and 5-year Treasury notes was only +0.07 from 1926 to 2013. That's useful to know because it confirms that, over very long time spans, stocks and bonds will perform on their own, mostly unrelated, cycles.

Just be advised that while correlation makes for interesting data, in the short- and mid-term it does not predict behavior. There is no assurance that average long-term correlations will hold for any given point in time. Why? Because asset correlations are dynamic: they fluctuate constantly.

Asset Class Details
Let's explore the characteristics of the different major asset classes:

Stocks, of all kinds, have historically been the best long-term investment. Going forward, there is the possibility of fading U.S. economic leadership, so I make a substantial commitment to **international stocks** too. For my purposes in retirement living, I don't make a distinction between growth/value or large/medium/small cap stocks. I don't think the differences in correlation warrant managing different investments. I own broad-based funds of all stocks – domestic and international – and I'm done with it.

Stocks are the workhorses of your portfolio. They can deliver the long-term returns that will keep your financial base growing and ahead of inflation. But they are temperamental steeds: You need to protect them in bad times with a fortress of more conservative holdings – bonds and cash at a minimum.

There are many types of **bonds** to choose from: I lean toward higher-quality, short- and intermediate-term government and corporate issues. But I see nothing wrong with holding longer-term, lower-quality bonds as a small portion of a diversified bond fund.

What about *international* bonds? Only recently has it been possible to buy these in low-cost index funds. Now they've started appearing as recommended components of balanced portfolios. So far, I have not seen the need to incorporate international bonds into my own portfolio. I suspect that the diversification to be had will be less than what I already get by holding international stocks.

Real estate has been a traditional store of wealth, with low correlation to the stock market. However, it can easily fail my criteria for liquidity, low transaction costs, low cost of ownership, and minimal expertise. Unless you are handy at home maintenance, and a committed property manager, the solution is simple: Buy real estate or REIT mutual funds or ETFs.

In general, **commodities**, like gold, have been a speculative game, because they don't generate income or growth, meaning they produce no real (after inflation) returns, in theory. Rather, you make money by selling them at a higher price at a later time in the economic cycle. However, this somewhat simplistic view ignores a long-term trend in today's world: *scarcity*. Some rarer commodities in high demand will naturally increase in value over time. But whether they do or not, the facts of retirement – that you need to liquidate investments over arbitrary future economic cycles – dictate that you will very likely experience conditions where the sale of commodities could be profitable.

Then there is **cash**. It's the one asset class you must have on a daily basis, to live. And yet it is one of the least productive assets to hold. It can be critical for liquidity in a crisis, but you don't make a "killing" in cash alone. In my opinion, you hold enough cash that you can sleep at night, then you deploy all the rest of your assets in a range of asset classes that are likely to perform independently of each other. This gives you the best odds of being able to replenish your cash from something that is currently in favor.

Finally, there are a number of *exotic* asset classes that we've left out of this discussion: options, hedge funds, synthetic indexes, private equity, and collectibles, for example. In my opinion, these all fail the criteria for suitable asset classes for conservative retirement portfolios. Options, hedge funds, and synthetic indexes are complicated and expensive and lack transparency. Private equity and collectibles are illiquid. That doesn't mean you can't do well with some of these asset classes – you might, particularly if you have specialized knowledge. But you won't be able to take a passive approach to your investments, and the long-term odds will be against you.

So that leaves us with **six** candidate asset classes for early retirement portfolios. In my opinion and experience, these are the asset classes that careful investors should consider in retirement. Here is a rough idea of their historical returns and their possible behavior in different economic scenarios:

Table: Asset Class Returns and Behavior

Asset Class	Return	Growth	Recession	Inflation	Deflation
domestic stocks	10%	up	down	up	down
international stocks	9%	up	down	up	down
bonds	5%	up	flat	down	up
real estate	3%	up	down	up	down
gold/commodities	3%	flat	down	up	down
cash	<1%	flat	flat	down	up

Note: The returns shown here are very rough estimates, in round numbers, based on my reading and compositing of historical data. Different sources give different numbers for different time frames and slices of the market. These numbers include inflation, so you would need to subtract about 3% for the real return. Thus real estate and gold have produced minimal real return over the long haul, and cash has lost value! Also, there is no guarantee we'll see similar returns in the future. In fact, many experts are calling for *reduced* returns across nearly all asset classes going forward. Finally, the economy and its cycles are too complex for snap answers to the question of a how an asset class will behave under certain conditions. Nevertheless, I've taken a stab at some simple answers here, to acquaint you with the idea that asset classes likely *will* behave differently.

Asset Allocation

Asset allocation is one of the most important variables in your portfolio. The way you allocate your money to different *asset classes* will dictate the risk you take on. And it will likely prescribe the long-term returns you achieve.

Risk and reward enjoy an iron-clad relationship. You can't get more reward without taking on more risk. There is no magic asset class that can deliver more of the former, without also requiring more of the latter.

It isn't hard to find pundits who have back-tested some personal brew of asset classes to demonstrate they would have outperformed the market in the past. I don't dispute that asset allocation *will* dictate your returns. But I do question whether any of it can be predicted in advance.

How much of each asset class should you own? There are as many answers to that question as there are financial advisors and experts. The traditional approach is to estimate your "risk tolerance," perhaps with a questionnaire, and guess from that. Ultimately, in my opinion, the only reliable answer comes from personal experience in down markets.

I have favored a simple balanced portfolio for many years. Going into retirement, my investment portfolio was approximately 40% stocks, 40% bonds, 10% cash, and 10% gold. Of the stocks, approximately 15% were REIT's or real-estate related, and about 30% were international.

Are those allocations gospel? *No*. Are they right for you? *Not necessarily*. But they let me sleep easily at night, while providing adequate upside for most possible economic scenarios in my own retirement.

Retirement creates new urgency around the choice of asset classes. Now that I'm living off my assets full time, the value of holding potentially uncorrelated assets is crystal-clear. If diversification among asset classes was important to dampen volatility in your accumulation years, it's *even more* important in retirement.

If your investments are damaged, but you need them for living expenses in retirement, you can't necessarily wait for losses to be recovered. To bombproof your retirement income stream, you need a *mix* of asset classes that guarantees one or more winners in any possible economic scenario....

Managing Your Retirement Distributions

Regardless of which phase of the economic cycle currently reigns, and regardless of which asset allocation you choose, you will need to harvest a portion of your nest egg to cover your living expenses in retirement. How exactly should you go about living off your assets? This is another thorny retirement problem for which there seem to be as many answers as there are experts. Let's examine the options....

Withdrawal Strategies

Here is a high-level survey of all the many ways to withdraw from your nest egg in retirement. I'll cover every method or strategy that I'm aware of, from a general perspective. I'll also discuss what *I've* done, in early retirement.

By the end, you'll have a good, general sense of your retirement withdrawal options – both the positives and negatives. Every solution has its strengths, and its potential weaknesses. By understanding the possible approaches, then mixing them together into a personal solution, while remaining flexible and still accepting some risk, you can move forward and enjoy your retirement.

Fixed Withdrawals

Let's start with one of the simplest and therefore most popular withdrawal methods. That is withdrawing a **fixed** amount from your portfolio on a periodic basis. Typically, this is implemented by also adjusting for inflation annually, so the nominal amount actually grows over time, but remains constant in real terms. In other words, you are maintaining the same lifestyle from year to year.

If the amount you start with, in year one of your retirement, is 4% of your portfolio, then this is the classic 4% Rule, which we discussed earlier.

The advantages of the fixed withdrawal method are that it is relatively simple to implement. And it has been studied exhaustively, so you can easily find statistics on the survival probabilities for your portfolio, given a time span and asset allocation.

And this strategy is perfectly predictable – to a point. Your lifestyle is "locked in." You know much you have to spend each year. *Unless your money runs out.*

That is the chief drawback of the fixed withdrawal strategy. Nobody can say for sure how long your money will last. Yes, studies based on historical data show it could last for 30 years. But history may not repeat. And, unless you implement some kind of annual review, you will have no flexibility to make your money last longer, if needed. Nor will you be able to deal with emergency expenses, or enjoy splurges if your portfolio is doing well.

Variable Withdrawals
If you don't withdraw a fixed amount from your portfolio every year, then it stands to reason you'll be withdrawing a **variable** amount. But there are many formulas for computing that fluctuating withdrawal. Let's review them.

You could withdraw a **fixed percentage** of your portfolio every year. Say you chose to withdraw exactly 5% of your portfolio every January, regardless of its current value or how the market had performed. This is the

endowment withdrawal approach. The great advantage of this is that it automatically builds some flexibility into your withdrawals as a function of market performance. If the market is up, your fixed percentage will be a larger sum. If the market is down, it will be smaller. Even better, you will *never* run out of money! Because you are always withdrawing some percent of your portfolio, it can never be wiped out, mathematically speaking. That sounds great until you look at the downside: Your portfolio could get very *small*! So your lifestyle will fluctuate, perhaps dramatically, over the long term. Lastly, although this withdrawal strategy is variable, it isn't truly flexible, because the *market*, not you, controls the size of the annual withdrawals.

For another approach to a market-based withdrawal percentage, there are **market valuation**-based strategies. These advocate that you actually withdraw *less* when markets are high, because the projected returns going forward will be lower.

Yet another approach to variable withdrawals is to base the sum on your **life expectancy**. In its simplest form, each year you would withdraw one divided by your remaining life expectancy in years. (For a simple source of life expectancy data, see the IRS RMD tables.) So if your life expectancy is 30 years, you'd withdraw 1/30 or about 3.3% in the current year. This approach has intuitive appeal. You are dividing your money up evenly according to how many years you expect to remain living. And that expectation is updated annually based on statistics. Again, you will never run out of money! But again, there is no guarantee exactly how *much* money you'll have in your last years. Unfortunately, if you consider how the denominator in that formula works, along with the potential for asset growth, you'll likely wind up with smaller withdrawals in early retirement, and possibly large withdrawals later. That's a negative in my view: Instead of "front loading" withdrawals so that you spend more in your early years when you have a greater chance of being alive, and are healthy to enjoy it, you are likely to "back load" the withdrawal process, saving too much until the end.

To allow for more generous withdrawals up front, plus potential flexibility, yet institute some safety measures, you can use a modified variable withdrawal strategy consisting of a fixed percentage with some **bounds or guardrails**. There are more modern versions of this strategy, but one of the first and simplest approaches came from Bob Clyatt in his groundbreaking book on early retirement, *Work Less, Live More*. He calls his approach the "95% Rule." You start by calculating 4% of your portfolio value every year. Then, to accommodate bad market years, you can withdraw either that 4% amount, or 95% of the amount you withdrew the *previous* year, whichever is larger. That means you never have to cut your lifestyle more than 5% in any given year. Clyatt reports that there is minimal impact on portfolio success rates – generally just a few percentage points – from using his 95% Rule. So it lets you "smooth" changes in your lifestyle, while taking little additional risk of running out of money.

While variable withdrawal strategies are among the most complex retirement income solutions for an individual to implement, annuities are probably the simplest....

Annuity Payments

What if you want even more retirement guarantees? On the surface, **annuities** – which we covered in section 2 – appear to solve almost all the problems of fixed and variable withdrawals.

An annuity offers income payments for life. That eliminates the possibility of outliving your assets, as long as the insurance company remains solvent. Annuities get high points for consistency. But that's also their chief drawback. They are inflexible. You lose access to your principal. If you die early, you will likely have left quite a bit of money on the table. If you have an emergency and need a lump sum of money, you probably can't get it. You may not be able to pass on wealth to your children. Only if you live a long time, and your expenses stay relatively constant, does an annuity pay off.

And that's assuming *inflation* remains tame. With an annuity in retirement, we're talking two, three, or four decades of cash flow. Is it inflation adjusted? Inflation can be a big deal over such time spans. And, today at least, inflation-adjusted annuities are hard to find, and feature minuscule payouts. (Looking at my latest inflation-adjusted annuity quote, I'd rather take my chances in the markets.)

Flexible Capital Preservation

We've discussed fixed and variable withdrawals, and annuity payments. These are all relatively static, idealized, or inflexible systems for withdrawing from assets in retirement. They make good scenarios for running simulations and performing academic research.

Now let me discuss what I think most people actually tend to *do* in retirement, at least early retirement. And, this is also what *I'm* doing, until I see better ideas and a more complete picture.

I call this *Flexible Capital Preservation* – living off **interest**, **dividends**, **growth**, and some **part-time work** income, all with an eye to preserving assets. This is, in my view, the only sensible strategy for *early retirement*, where there are still decades of uncertainty yawning in front of you. If you retire in your 50's or earlier, with no inflation-adjusted pension in sight, it is simply unwise to draw down your assets in any significant way. The goal should be to preserve (though not necessarily grow) your net worth, keeping your gunpowder dry until you are much further down the road.

How does this work in practice? Well, if your assets are large enough, or the markets are strong enough, you can afford to spend only your annual dividends and growth each year. If that isn't the case, then you will need to work part-time, possibly leveraging your relative financial independence to create a lifestyle business that supplements your investment income, while not detracting from your quality of life.

Many of us will use Flexible Capital Preservation, or a hybrid solution, throughout retirement. The other withdrawal strategies described above have drawbacks.

Some can't guarantee that you won't run out of money: You could die broke. Some can't guarantee your lifestyle: You could be living out of a trailer and eating cereal in your later years. Some don't guarantee principal: You might not have any money available for emergencies, and you might not have any left to pass on to your heirs. Some require active involvement and financial management: You or a spouse must be able and interested.

Despite all those drawbacks, the biggest problem with most of the withdrawal systems is precisely that they are artificial *systems*. Ask yourself if it is really possible to maintain *any* "system" consistently for the 20- to 40-year time span of a modern retirement? I'm highly organized about my financial life, but my "system" changes regularly. Much as we'd like to trust in a single approach, things change.

I'm pessimistic that there will ever be a perfect, turnkey, "just tell me what to do" retirement income solution. Most of us are going to pick and choose from the options, combining them in an attempt to harvest most of the benefits, while minimizing the liabilities and preserving our flexibility. In many cases we'll use annuities to create a guaranteed income floor, plus investment portfolios for recreation, emergencies, and legacy. And that will be good enough for a secure and comfortable retirement.

Asset Class Strategies
So far in discussing withdrawal strategies, we've been assuming you'd pull from all your *asset classes* in equal proportions, without regard for factors like the economic cycle or recent performance. That's a typical "Total

Returns" approach used by most passive index investors. So, for example, if you are invested 40% in stocks and 60% in bonds, and need $40,000 for the year, you would sell $16,000 of stocks and $24,000 of bonds to meet your needs.

Most of us know we can't outperform the market by actively trading stocks. Our best bet for building wealth over the long haul is to invest regularly in low-cost, broad-based index funds. Trying to time the market by actively trading has been thoroughly debunked. But how does that lesson apply in retirement, when we *must* choose when and how to liquidate our accumulated assets?

To me, it makes no sense to live off your conservative cash and bond buckets when stock markets are up. That's like dipping into the storehouse when there is fresh, healthy grain available in the fields. Much better to be selling volatile equity assets when they are in favor, and to preserve your safe assets for the bad times. Shouldn't that make your savings last longer, or allow you to spend more, or both?

The answer seems obvious. *But, how do you choose your most valuable assets to sell?*

I set out to answer that question using a computer model and historical market returns to analyze different withdrawal strategies for the major asset classes – stocks and bonds. Altogether, I tested six different possible strategies for retirement withdrawals and several hundred different scenarios. My research showed that keeping it simple and using a consistent, value-driven approach could mean extracting millions more income from your nest egg over the course of a long retirement.

The strategies themselves were each quite simple, but varied significantly in their philosophy and results. Initially, they were pure *withdrawal* strategies. They never bought or sold, or changed the asset allocation, other than to generate the required withdrawal in a given year. Later, I added rebalancing. For each strategy I computed the *success rate* – how many of the historical retirement periods ended with a portfolio balance greater than zero, and the *median ending portfolio value*

Detailed results and updates to the research are posted on my blog. I'll just share the major conclusions here:

- The results were striking. They showed a difference in success rate of more than 15%, and a difference in ending portfolio value of more than $4M, based solely on *how* you withdraw from the major asset classes.

- *Consistency* is most important. Reliably following my top, valuation-driven strategies will likely beat the lower-performing, momentum-inspired moving average strategies. And those top retirement withdrawal strategies will almost surely trounce any emotion-driven attempts at market timing.

- The most successful strategy I tested uses one of the most widely studied and watched stock valuation indicators – Robert Shiller's Cyclically Adjusted Price-to-Earnings ratio or CAPE (defined as the price of the S&P 500 divided by the average of the last ten years' earnings, adjusted for inflation). The strategy simply withdraws from stocks when the CAPE is greater than its long-term median (a kind of average), and it withdraws entirely from bonds when the CAPE is below its long-term median. Variations on this strategy occupied the top three slots in my results for success rate, and the two top slots for ending portfolio value.

- The data reminds us of a general principle when progressing from higher to lower stock allocations: Holding more stocks generally increases your success rate, and your ending portfolio value. But it also increases volatility. Likewise, the unmodified CAPE Median strategy produced higher average stock allocations, along with higher success rates and ending portfolio values. The odds are for coming out ahead, but it may be a bumpier ride!

- One strategy for smoothing out that ride is to add *rebalancing*. Contrary to conventional wisdom, rebalancing is *not* about juicing performance (helping you to buy low and sell high). Annual rebalancing assumes that last year's outperformance should be liquidated, but in fact we know that most stock market trends last far longer than one year. Rebalancing is actually about *reducing risk*. In my simulations, adding rebalancing always reduced volatility (stock allocation), at the price of reducing the ending value, while having relatively little impact on success rates.

Note: When it comes to investing, never forget that *past performance is no guarantee of future results*. Though a strategy of selling assets at cyclical highs makes logical sense, and my historical simulations seem to support it, there is simply no guarantee that what worked in the past will continue to work in the future. One expert felt my findings for CAPE were similar to *tactical asset allocation*, mostly explained by the increased stock exposure, and that I may have oversimplified my treatment of the median. While the technical details can always be debated, there is a lot to learn from modeling, as long as we don't take the results as gospel. For those who want to dig deeper, or implement their own withdrawal strategies, there are detailed explanations of the different strategies I studied, along with technical discussion, critiques, and any updates to my research, on <u>my blog</u>.

Cash Flow

Once you've decided where the cash for retirement living expenses is to come from, how to do you actually dole it out to yourself on a monthly basis?

Look to your own personal organizational style. Mine is ad hoc: Once or twice a year, when I need money, I sell some of our most appreciated assets. I track all our expenses in Quicken. Weekly, I enter receipts and bills and reconcile statements. So, I always know within a few dollars how we are doing against our budget, and can make course corrections if needed. Tracking as we go works well for us, since our accounts are fully automated.

Some people are more comfortable with a "paycheck" model for managing their spending. In this approach, you decide on the annual amount you can withdraw, then set up a monthly mechanism (ideally, at no charge) to have assets sold and the proceeds transferred into your checking account for regular expenses. You then "save" unused amounts from this account for major or unexpected expenses. Since you have the money in an account somewhere anyway, there is no real financial need for this approach – it's simply a bookkeeping mechanism. But, it may be the simplest and safest way for many.

As for the actual accounts, we keep our main checking at USAA, essentially an online bank. The majority of our investments are at Vanguard, and Schwab (where I keep another checking account). I wouldn't fault anybody for consolidating everything at one institution, for simplicity. But I like spreading the responsibility around, so I always have a functional account if there is fraud or a computer glitch.

In short, there is no right or wrong way to do it. The key thing is living to a budget, in one form or another, and implementing it in a way that suits you, and your spouse.

"Buckets"

Some financial advisors push the idea of *buckets* as a solution to the retirement cash management problem. The concept has intuitive appeal: You segregate your retirement assets into several categories or "buckets" according to their volatility, and when you'll need them. So you have a short-term bucket of cash, a medium-term bucket of bonds, and a long-term bucket of stocks. This sounds sophisticated, logical, and reassuring to clients. But, it's really just a different lens for viewing a traditional asset allocation: Is there really any difference between saying you have 10% cash and 30% bonds in your asset allocation, versus saying you have a 10% short-term "bucket" and a 30% medium-term "bucket"?

In theory with this system, there is some method for moving assets between buckets, so that you always have a reserve and never have to sell at a loss. But, the decisions about when to sell equity assets to replenish cash and bond buckets are the same as for other strategies, and just as difficult. At least two prominent researchers (Jim Otar and Moshe Milevsky) have analyzed the buckets strategy and found that no systematic method exists! In most cases, the strategy simply dissolves into a kind of lopsided total returns approach. If not careful, over time you wind up with most of your money in the riskier asset. The end result is that you overperform, or underperform, a total returns approach – depending on market conditions. At best, on average, the performance is about the same.

My own research also indicates that cash/bond buckets are overrated. Refilling buckets reduces to the same problem I investigated: when and how to sell equity assets. Rather than stockpiling asset classes in buckets, it may be just as effective to simply sell whichever one (stocks/bonds) is in favor, on demand. Though, personally, I will probably always keep at least a year of cash living expenses on hand in retirement.

Watching Your Retirement Fuel Gauge

Now that we've discussed economic cycles, asset classes, and managing the distributions from your nest egg, let's talk about monitoring just how you and your assets are doing in retirement. While we can't make this quite as simple as the fuel gauge in a car, the idea is the same. You want a readout on your retirement that tells you, as effectively as possible, whether your money is holding out, or whether you need to take action. But, before we do that, let's briefly review the math behind portfolio losses and distributions....

The Mathematics of Loss

If you lose 10% on your investments one year, how much do you need to make next year just to get back to even? The answer is *more than* 10%, because you now have less capital to work with. In fact, with only 90% of your original capital, you now need to make slightly more than 11% to get back where you started: (10/90)*100.

Perhaps that doesn't sound too bad. But what about more serious losses of say 30%, or 50%? (Remember 2008-2009.) Well, it turns out you need to make about **43%** to recover from a 30% loss, and an astounding **100%** to recover from a 50% loss! Getting those kinds of market returns over a short time span is about as likely as winning the lottery!

So you simply cannot afford to take substantial portfolio losses as you approach retirement. But the issue is even more serious than that. Because, once you begin *distributions* from a portfolio in retirement, it becomes even *less* resilient to losses. A sideways market, one that fluctuates up and down within a range for years, can produce modest returns in an **accumulation** portfolio. But, as we've discussed with the "time value of fluctuations" in section 2, it's generally bad news for a **distribution** portfolio.

A distribution portfolio is far more fragile, far less likely to grow, than an accumulation portfolio – because, regardless of what the markets do, it is always under stress from your regular withdrawals. You must *sell* more shares when prices are low, just to support the same standard of living. Once you sell those shares to live on, you are "locking in" losses. That money is gone and can never earn for you again. And those losses erode your working capital at a disturbing clip....

Here's a simple example: Suppose we encounter a run-of-the-mill bear market, a 20% decline. Given the mathematics of loss, you'd need to make 25% the next year to break even. But what if you are *living off* your portfolio at the same time, withdrawing at the supposedly "safe" 4% rate? Now you need to make back *about 32%*, instead of that already-daunting 25%. Withdrawing from a portfolio during a down market, you can very rapidly dig a hole from which you'll never escape....

Watching for Trouble
Early in retirement, market fluctuations will dwarf your withdrawals at first. It's like sailing a small boat in a storm at sea. You are tossed up and down as one giant wave arrives after another, and it's very difficult to detect whether your progress is *forwards*, *backwards*, or *sideways*. This phenomenon makes it extremely difficult to understand the

impact of your own withdrawals. It's hard to see whether you are on track or not.

But, as we've discussed, based on current research, unless your annual expenses are less than about 2% to 3% of your portfolio, you must exercise caution. If so, what are the warning signs that your portfolio could be in trouble?

When I retired a while back, with little specific knowledge of how to manage a distribution portfolio, I had a couple of simple warning signs in mind. We had set aside two years of cash for the start of my retirement, so a **two-year horizon** seemed sensible.

I figured if our net worth went down in the first year, I'd start keeping an eye on things. If another year passed, and our net worth went down again, that would be enough warning to trigger some action. Either we'd cut our living expenses significantly, or I would ramp up my part-time work efforts.

As it turns out, we didn't hit that warning level. In fact, our portfolio grew during the first few years of my retirement. And I've learned that a two-year window is a bit conservative. You'd better be prepared to see your net worth go down for more than a couple of years, especially when you are no longer accumulating assets, because, as we've seen, the average length of a bear market cycle is three years, and could go as long as nine!

I also had in mind another simple warning signal that would require a response on my part: **being forced to sell at a loss**. The game plan was never to sell *any* investment for less than I paid. If I did, that would indicate things were going badly. Perhaps that's true, but it's not a practical indicator: With half our portfolio in short- and medium-term bonds, we could go nearly half our retirement with very little likelihood of selling at a loss. But, that would by no means ensure success for the second half, if our equities didn't eventually perform!

Better Warning Signs

I've since learned of several more sophisticated, though still not foolproof, approaches to this problem of knowing whether you're starting to run out of money in retirement....

Let's begin with the **withdrawal rate** itself. We've reviewed the studies and discussed this issue at length. In virtually no case does anybody recommend a safe withdrawal rate **over 5%** early in retirement. So that is one simple warning sign: if your annual withdrawal rate should approach 5% at the start of a 30- to 40-year retirement, you are almost *surely* in trouble. But note that the reverse is *not* true: Just because your withdrawal rate is below 5%, doesn't mean that you're *not* in trouble!

That's because, as we've learned, current **market valuations** as reflected by the Cyclically Adjusted Price-to-Earnings ratio (CAPE), are a reasonably reliable indicator of retirement portfolio success. As I write this, CAPE is in the mid 20's – high by historical standards. This means there is a statistical tendency for reduced market returns going forward from today. So that is another warning sign: If the CAPE is well above its historical average when you retire, consider yourself on notice. (You can follow the CAPE/Shiller PE for yourself at Multpl.com.)

The final warning signal I'll discuss is related to my earlier two-year threshold, but has a stronger basis in research. It's the **"Fourth-Year Check-Up"** presented in Jim Otar's *Unveiling the Retirement Myth*.

Otar derived this warning signal by calculating the values of numerous retirement portfolios for each possible historical retirement period, starting in 1900. He looked at those values after four years of retirement, and then again after 20 years. And he found that the winners after four years had a much higher survival rate in the long run. (Though he did use higher than usual withdrawal rates in his analysis, which makes for a conservative test.)

The Fourth-Year Check-Up signal is very easy to monitor, as long as you already track your net worth or total portfolio value. You simply compare that value on the fourth anniversary of your retirement, to the original number when you retired: *Is it more or less?* If less, this is an indication that the sequence of market returns has been working against you, and there is now a higher probability of running out of money. The good news would be that you are only four years into your retirement, so you could still have some flexibility and options for improving your situation.

In summary, the dangers to a distribution portfolio are far more severe than those to an accumulation portfolio. Fortunately, there are some simple warning signs you can check to know if you're on track. Unfortunately, they aren't entirely accurate, and some could be too conservative for your situation, leading you to work longer, spend less, or annuitize too much. But, if you place a high value on not running out of money or reducing your lifestyle in retirement, you will heed these warnings....

Table: **Your Retirement Fuel Gauge**

Indicator	Warning Level
sale of securities	at a loss
withdrawal rate	greater than 5%
market valuations	CAPE greater than historical average
four-year check-up	portfolio lower than first year

What If You're Running Low?

Running out of money before you run out of life. It's the biggest fear many retirees face. And, for baby boomers and succeeding generations without guaranteed pensions, it's not just a night terror – it's a realistic concern. Without adequate savings, a prudent lifestyle, and regular financial checkups, running low in retirement is a very real possibility.

If that happens, what do you do? At the simplest level there are two solutions:

1. Reduce your expenses

2. Increase your income

Like it or not, *reducing expenses*, living more modestly, is the medicine that many retirees will take at some point in their future. It's the solution most under our control, and the one we'll have to accept if there are no other choices. The main question is whether you'll do it on your terms – gradually, while preserving what's most important to you, or whether you'll have it forced on you by events.

I recommend doing as much cutting *before retirement* as possible, while you are still working. That way you can get accustomed to a modest lifestyle, and make adjustments while you still have the options offered by a steady income. Also, the lower your expenses are while you are still working, the more you can save for retirement, and the sooner you can retire.

The second solution, *increasing your income*, has several facets. First and most obviously, you could simply return to your career or work longer. But, as we've discussed, that is a more reasonable option for *early* retirees than *traditional* retirees. You could also attempt to increase the investment return on your savings. If your portfolio is overly conservative – largely in cash, CDs, or bonds – you could allocate more to stocks. But trying to increase returns beyond a reasonable allocation to stocks is a dangerous game. You might bail out at a loss when the going gets tough. And it *will* get tough. Because, it is impossible to consistently outperform the stock market without taking on more volatility and risk. In other words, to possibly outperform the market, you have to take on more risk of *underperforming* the market – which could mean running out of money even sooner in retirement.

There are better options. Next we'll discuss the retirement *lifeboat strategies*. These are your last resort and also one of your most powerful tools for developing confidence in making the retirement decision. They give you an *action plan* to continue living a comfortable life, even if the worst economic scenarios come to pass in your retirement....

The Lifeboat Strategies

When I retired at age 50, I couldn't really be certain that we would have enough money to live comfortably for the next 30-40 years, or longer. Yes, I ran a bevy of retirement calculators. But that's a long time into the future for any prediction to hold true. So, what really gave me confidence to retire early was not the calculations, but having a *backup plan*. I knew if things didn't go as expected, there would be something I could do about it.

The lifeboat strategies are backup plans that can generate the baseline income you need to cover your essential living expenses. That's the minimum you need for food, shelter, utilities, and medical care and not much else other than free, frugal fun. You hope retirement never comes to that, but, as we've discussed, it's virtually impossible to achieve complete certainty about life decades down the road.

It's best to plan for and expect the high percent of outcomes that allow you more comfort and luxury in retirement, and also be prepared for a certain percent that don't. If you've thought in advance about how you could gracefully transition to a reduced lifestyle, chances are you would be able to do it with minimal impact on your overall happiness, should circumstances require it.

To be effective, the lifeboat strategies must make a dramatic difference in either your *cost of living* or your *income*. Enough of a difference that you could compensate for a major economic dislocation. All of these strategies come down to dramatically reducing your withdrawal rate against your savings, if conditions require it, for some period of time in your retirement.

A key aspect of the strategies, as I'm defining them here, is that they need to be *entirely under your control*. You can't depend on good fortune, the benevolence of others, or external economic conditions, in the worst-case scenarios. For this reason, we won't be discussing either *working* or *inheritances* here. Maybe you could work some in retirement. Or maybe you can count on inheriting some family wealth, eventually. But work requires a cooperative economy and employer. And inheritances are dictated by the life span and spending habits of others. Don't pin your baseline retirement comfort on factors you can't control.

Expense Strategies

Let's discuss cutting expenses first. Reducing expenses, living more modestly, is the solution most under our control, and the one we'll have to accept if there are no other choices. It's far more realistic for most people to cut expenses than it is to drum up more income in retirement, especially traditional retirement. There are two primary expense-cutting strategies that meet our lifeboat criteria. Each you can implement entirely on your own:

Cutting Discretionary Spending

Let's start with *discretionary spending....*

Could you cut your retirement living budget by a significant 10% to 25% if necessary in bad years? I know we could. That's because about 20% of our retirement budget is "recreation" – dining out, entertainment, gear, and travel.

We could live without these for a period, without suffering greatly.

We love to eat out, but we can get just as much enjoyment from preparing delicious, healthy food at home and "dining out" on our back patio. Our main entertainment expense is watching first-run movies at the nearby theater. But we could live without those, while enjoying the seemingly infinite catalog of older movies and TV shows in our *Amazon Prime* subscription. I like using the best outdoor gear, and we've upgraded significantly in our early retirement. But, at this point, we are well outfitted for a lifetime of cycling, hiking, climbing, and camping adventures. As for traveling, we'll never stop completely, but we could cut back significantly by reducing the *distance* of our trips. There are numerous attractions within a half-day's drive of our current ideal retirement location. We could also eliminate fancier accommodations in favor of RV camping, which we love anyway.

How about you? Can you identify your largest discretionary expenses and prepare yourself to live without them, if necessary, for a while in retirement? If, like us, recreation is your largest category, then realize how much leverage you have over this expense: The key is to create a lifestyle that is inherently recreational, without any required extra expenses. Live in a beautiful location that offers free or cheap opportunities outdoors. Walk or ride bikes. Hold potluck dinners with friends and stream movies over the Internet. If you set up your life intelligently, then having to live this way for a few years while the economy is down would be no hardship. In fact, it could even be fun! (It sounds like the college years to me, and those were some of the best of my life.) The change in routine could be the perfect prescription to invigorate your retirement!

You can be happy with less. Surveys of actual experience show that <u>most retirees are happy</u>, even though they are generally living on much less than they did while working. The average replacement rate – the percent of previous income needed once retired – for today's retirees may be as low as 60%. Not only are work and family-related expenses gone once you retire, but you may be done keeping up with the Joneses too. In one <u>study</u>, 85% of recently retired households confirmed that they don't need to spend as much as they did before retirement to be satisfied.

In my experience, people are tempted to spend more on things and entertainment to ease the pain of jobs and careers that no longer provide meaning in their lives. Transition into retirement, and the need for such spending on surrogate painkillers goes away.

Downsizing

The second expense strategy, one of the biggest levers that most people can throw in their retirement, relates to *shelter*.

If you live in a McMansion, you can downsize to a modest house. If you live in a house, you can downsize to a townhome, cabin, or condo. If you live in one of those, you can downsize to an apartment. If you live in an apartment, you can downsize to an RV. (Comfortable, dignified RV living costs so little that it is available to virtually anyone who has managed to put away $10-$20K in equity for a used rig, and worked long enough to get Social Security and

Medicare.) And if none of those options work, you can take in a boarder, or explore retiring overseas, where less-developed countries sport large retiree populations, all the amenities – including good health care – and a substantially lower cost of living.

For a simple but common example, consider that many prospective retirees own half-million-dollar homes in popular neighborhoods near the coasts or in the big cities. By contrast, it's entirely possible to own an attractive two-bedroom house or condo in a smaller town with a beautiful setting for $200K. Don't believe it? Search Zillow.com for lovely *Pagosa Springs Colorado*, where we recently visited. As I write this, I count 30 properties with at least two bedrooms in or near downtown, for under $200K.

In this example, downsizing would net you about $300K. That could be used to generate more retirement income. At a 4% withdrawal rate, available by annuitizing if not by safe withdrawals, the downsizing transition nets you **$1K/month** in extra retirement income!

What if you don't own a large home in an affluent neighborhood? Regardless of your financial status, most people can dramatically reduce their cost of shelter, if needed. In their book *The Clash of Generations*, Scott Burns and Laurence Kotlikoff show that a retiring middle-income couple can increase their annual spending by more than $13,000/year by selling their home and becoming renters. And, if they become fulltime RVers, they can boost spending by another $10,000/year. That's a lot of cash that could go towards maintaining or improving the rest of your lifestyle, simply by downsizing your home.

Would these shelter choices be unwelcome for some? Possibly. But that perception is entirely under your own control. In many cases, it's simply a matter of relocating to a less expensive area – nothing else about your lifestyle needs to change. There is an almost infinite supply of potential locations and homes in the world. Surely, one has the right conditions for your happiness? Relocation is a modest sacrifice, given that it could ensure your financial survival.

Income Strategies

Next we'll discuss the few ways you can increase your retirement income safely and independently. These are more difficult. As mentioned, we are ruling out returning to work because that generally requires a cooperative economy or employer. Also, working may not be physically possible for traditional retirees. We are also ruling out trying to increase the return on your savings, because of the risk you'll do more harm than good to your assets.

Fortunately, you can still access a couple of powerful and safe income-enhancement strategies. But, they carry a critical prerequisite: You *must* have some assets – either investments or a home – to begin:

Annuitizing

The first strategy for safely increasing retirement income is to purchase a fixed annuity. I prefer the plain vanilla single premium immediate annuity. As we've discussed, with this type of contract, you pay the insurance company a lump sum, and they then pay you monthly income for life. There is no variability – no "upside" or "downside" – in the income stream, other than perhaps inflation adjustments, if you pay for those. And costs are easy to assess, because you know precisely what you'll pay, and precisely what you'll get back, and when.

Fixed annuities are generally invested in bonds, yet they can pay more than the going rate on a typical bond fund. That is, they can substantially increase your investment income over what you could accomplish with your own investments, given a similar level of risk.

The first reason is simple: An annuity returns some of your principal to you, along with interest payments. That means you are consuming principal. When you purchase an annuity, you give up control over your principal and, in return, the insurance company returns portions of it to you over time to increase returns. But, you probably won't get it all back unless you live longer than expected.

The second reason that an annuity can enhance returns is more complex. It's called "mortality credits" – the technical term for the benefit you get by pooling your money with a large group of other people.

Individuals don't know their lifetime in advance. If you're managing money on your own, you must spend conservatively to ensure you don't run out. By contrast, an insurance company can know very accurately the statistical lifetimes of a large group. That means the company can pay everybody a better income than they could afford on their own, confident that some individuals will die earlier than average, leaving assets to pay the incomes of those who live longer.

Add up both of these factors and you get a powerful result: When you purchase an annuity, you can usually increase your safe investment income yield by *several percentage points*, depending on your age. As a rough example, consider that as I write this, the SEC Yield on Vanguard's Intermediate-Term Bond Index Fund (VBIIX) is about 2.5%. Yet ImmediateAnnuities.com reports that an equally safe fixed immediate annuity can pay a 65-year-old couple about 5.7% – more than 3% higher.

So, your liquid assets, whatever they may be, can go much further in providing retirement income as an annuity. Just remember that an annuity is not like your other investments. You don't have access to your principal. So the downside is significant if you must put most of your assets into one. It reduces or eliminates your cash reserve for dealing with unexpected expenses or leaving a legacy. However, your heirs would probably prefer that you be self-supporting, even if it means they lose out on an inheritance. And an annuity can be instrumental in achieving that primary objective – baseline retirement security.

Reverse Mortgages
What if your investment assets are minimal or you've already maximized your income from annuities? Is there somewhere else you can turn to produce more retirement income? Yes, if you own or have substantial equity in your house, there is. It's a somewhat complex and checkered financial product that has recently become more palatable. As noted retirement researcher Wade Pfau writes, "…recent research has demonstrated how financially responsible

individuals can improve their retirement sustainability with a *reverse mortgage*."

A reverse mortgage lets you generate income from your home equity, guaranteed for life as long as you stay in the home. You, or your heirs, may not own your home in the end, but you'll never owe more on the loan than the value of your home. Government insurance protects you if the bank has problems producing income, and it protects the bank if you should consume all your equity before dying. From your perspective, the advantage is clear: Using only your home, without requiring any additional assets, you now have access to an income stream that will last as long as you do.

Though recent reforms have reduced the costs and risks, reverse mortgages are far from a perfect solution. In my opinion, they should be considered a last resort. In the right circumstances, they are a legitimate choice, but they remain complex, and expensive. They are sometimes sold aggressively in inappropriate situations. Used recklessly, they could result in losing your home. Why? Because you still must have cash flow available to pay for taxes, insurance, and maintenance – or risk default.

Given the expense and downside, the government requires financial counseling before you can take on a reverse mortgage. The transaction costs in a reverse mortgage are similar to buying a home. At settlement there will be an origination fee (shop around for the best deal: only the *maximum* is set by the government), an upfront mortgage insurance premium (generally 0.5% of the appraised value), and other typical real estate closing costs.

Then, for the life of the loan, the lender will draw down your home equity to pay its interest charge based on the market rate, an FHA insurance premium of 1.25%, and possibly a servicing charge. Those long-term charges will substantially erode your wealth, though the effects may be hidden by the regular income you receive.

In my example calculations, about 5% to 7% of available home equity disappears into fees at the start of a reverse mortgage. Then there are the monthly charges compounding for the life of the loan after that. If there is a cheaper way you can generate retirement income than a reverse mortgage, you should choose it instead. My figures show a reverse mortgage generating about a 3% draw against your total home equity for life, not adjusted for inflation. Compared to getting *zero*, that's pretty good. But compared to annuitizing, or probable stock market returns, it's nothing special.

The next big downside to a reverse mortgage is the *complexity*. The more complicated a financial instrument, the harder it is to determine the risk and reward. You may have to rely heavily on mortgage professionals to understand and compare offerings. I found two online calculators useful in the process, from the Mortgage Professor and the National Reverse Mortgage Lenders Association (NRMLA).

Despite the drawbacks, reverse mortgages will likely be the best retirement income solution for baby boomers who are "house poor" – stuck in large homes with inadequate cash flow. Downsizing would often be preferable, but reverse mortgages are another option. Scott Burns writes, "Used for long term planning rather than emergencies, reverse mortgages are likely to become a major tool for the millions of Americans who have a lot more equity in their homes than in their retirement savings."

The essence of the lifeboat strategies for increasing retirement *income* is this: You give away some or all of your *principal* in exchange for better cash flow. That also means that you lose some flexibility – for handling emergency expenses, gifting, or inheritance. But, in return, you get the peace of mind of guaranteed income for life.

Income Strategy Example

How do these income-based strategies work in practice? For a typical retired couple, what is the potential financial benefit of annuitizing and taking out a reverse mortgage? To answer these questions, let's analyze a simple scenario....

Assume a couple, both age 65, are concerned about their ability to meet retirement expenses going forward. They have $500K in total saved investment assets, and they own their $250K home free and clear.

For an initial retirement income strategy, they try systematic withdrawals from their investments using a safe withdrawal rate of 3%. At that rate, this couple's $500K in investments can safely generate about $1,250/month in inflation-adjusted retirement income. Coupled with Social Security, that might be enough, but it could be very tight, depending on their lifestyle. What if they want or need more, and are willing to give up some control of their principal?

As I write this, ImmediateAnnuities.com will let them buy an annuity with those investment assets that generates about $2,400/month. And the NRMLA reverse mortgage calculator shows they can take out a reverse mortgage on their home to generate about another $700/month for life. That's a total of about $3,100/month in guaranteed retirement income.

So, by annuitizing plus using a reverse mortgage, this couple can nearly *triple* their available monthly retirement income versus what could be achieved using a safe withdrawal rate from their investments alone! By virtue of having some assets – investments and a home – and choosing to give up control over their principal, they can significantly boost their retirement income. And, though the final amount is not inflation-adjusted, it's likely to exceed what they could safely draw from their investments, for decades to come.

Take Action

- Keep an eye on simple metrics like the NBER business cycle and the CAPE, to understand roughly where you are in the current economic cycle. Are you seeing growth, inflation, recession, or deflation?

- Know the lengths of typical (3-year) and worst-case (9-year) bear markets, and set aside enough stable cash and bond assets to see you through any scenario.

- Review the six major uncorrelated asset classes, and decide on an appropriate asset allocation for your retirement portfolio.

- Understand the pros and cons of the different retirement withdrawal strategies. Rather than choosing one, identify *several* that you can blend into a hybrid strategy suiting your temperament and financial situation.

- Decide how you'll manage the cash flow for your retirement living expenses: Will you spend as needed and track the results to stay on budget, or will you issue yourself a regular retirement "paycheck" and save from that for irregular expenses?

- Monitor your *retirement fuel gauge*. If it issues *two* or more warning signs, it's time to take action!

- Review your available expense and income-based *lifeboat strategies*. How much could you save by cutting discretionary spending or downsizing? Get quotes online for an annuity, and a reverse mortgage. Understand the implications of these irrevocable financial moves, long before you need to make a decision.

CONCLUSION: YOUR RETIREMENT DECISION

"The only way most investors can drive their chance of success above 90% is to completely deprive themselves both before and after retirement. At some point, enough is enough – in order to live a little, you've got to bear some risk of failure." — William Bernstein

"From a certain point onward there is no longer any turning back. That is the point that must be reached." — Kafka

We've reviewed your retirement expenses and income. We've explored retirement math, run numbers to predict the future, and formulated plans for navigating your retirement journey, whatever may come.

Now, is it time for you to retire? Or, if not, when will be the right time?

If you've made it this far in the book, then you understand that there is no precise mathematical answer to that question.

Even a "professional" or a computer can't give you a definitive answer. They'd need data of course – details on your expenses, how your lifestyle will change over time, additional one-time expenses or income. Guesses would be made about market performance, tax rates, Social Security, health care, inflation. All of this data could then be jammed into a Monte Carlo simulation or historical analysis. And when the numbers came out, they might look impressive. But they wouldn't be any more accurate.

Nobody else can tell you with certainty if you have enough money to retire. There are so many unpredictable variables involved in the retirement equation, that a precise answer is impossible.

Given so many unknowns, *indecision* on your part is understandable, even normal.

Should you wait? Maybe things will be clearer when you're older. *Traditional* retirees may have more savings and are closer to Social Security, but their lifestyle and work options are more limited as well. And many older workers are forced to retire early for health or other reasons. *Early* retirees typically have more lifestyle flexibility, but less of a financial cushion, and many more years of retirement to finance, so their picture is unclear as well.

Even if you could develop an accurate retirement plan, could you implement it consistently over 30-40 years? Reality will always be a series of tactical decisions based on new events, logic, and emotion.

So, ultimately, with retirement, you have to make a *big decision* in the face of *uncertainty*. But, that's not so bad. Anybody who's gone to college, gotten married, raised children, or pursued a career, has already done that many times....

My Story, Continued…

At the start of this book, I told the story of my own early retirement decision. How I ran my numbers, then used an array of retirement calculators, and then read books and blogs from trusted and impartial voices. And how, once all the numbers were crunched, and compared, and analyzed, the general picture was that I could safely retire.

Did this process remove every trace of doubt in my mind? **No**. Considering the ongoing dramatic changes in the world, and that I was looking at a potential 40+ year retirement, that kind of confidence would be unjustified and foolhardy.

So what made the final difference in my decision? Ultimately, it was my desire to pursue a rewarding new part-time career, which turned into my blog and books. *I knew that producing value for others would give me a safety margin that no amount of planning or analysis could ever provide.* That commitment, plus the process described above and expanded on in the preceding pages of this book, gave me confidence to take the plunge.

And what has happened since my retirement? How has it gone for us? The news has been mixed, and not as planned. *No surprise there.* And we're doing just fine. *No surprise there.*

The market has generally grown since I retired in 2011, but all has not been roses. I hit my retirement savings goal before making the leap, yet, six months after I retired, our portfolio had been reduced by almost 10% thanks to stock market volatility. As I write this, the market has endured another correction. Meanwhile, one of my most respected financial sources continues to predict an economic catastrophe due to unresolved debt issues in the world.

The public university where our son won his substantial 4-year scholarship was in one of the states hardest hit by the Great Recession. To cope, the state legislature nearly *doubled* tuition during the course of his time there. A scholarship that should have been more than adequate for tuition, fees, and most of his living expenses, turned out to not even fully cover his tuition. He had to work harder, and we had to contribute more than expected. But he graduated, and we're still comfortably retired.

At this point, I expect our retirement portfolio to grow indefinitely. That's certainly the best and most comforting scenario. But we're prepared if it doesn't. We're diversified. We're prudent. We're flexible. We have an eye on our fuel gauge, and a lifeboat at hand if needed.

As planned, my wife, Caroline, worked another two years past my own retirement date, before retiring herself. She had stayed home for years while raising our son, and, when he was grown, she returned to teaching. She was a public school teacher in Tennessee, and loved her work, but it didn't pay much. I ran my retirement calculations assuming she wasn't working, so her income after I retired was a bonus for us. Now that she is retired, her pension is minimal, about $100/month, owing to her shortened career and cashing out along the way. But we *did* need her health benefits. And thanks to her retirement benefits, we have been able to buy into a group health plan at predictable rates.

A few years after I retired, we received a small inheritance, unexpectedly. It wasn't the kind of money that changes retirement outcomes, but it covered about a year of living expenses, which, along with Caroline's income, and a bull market, removed any immediate threats to our retirement savings. So we have been able to coast into the back half of our 50's with little fear of damaging our portfolio.

As a result, we've let our discretionary expenses creep higher: some extra travel and gear. All of those expenses were optional and could have been easily forgone, had times been harder.

Two years after I retired, because we were ready for new horizons, wanted to further remove any pressure from our portfolio in the early retirement years, and because it sounded like fun, we deployed our *downsizing lifeboat.* We sold our family home and lived out of our small RV for six months. We traveled across the country, following the seasons, staying near family and friends when possible, and getting to know different potential areas for relocating. Ultimately, we rented a nice two-bedroom townhome downtown in our ideal retirement location.

We've been here in Santa Fe for several years now. The surroundings that drew us are as beautiful and unique as ever. We've settled into a daily routine, made new friends, and established a network of contacts that make this feel like home, for now. Most days here still feel like we're "on vacation." Will we be here forever? Who knows? But, renting our home, and with our trusty camper van at the ready, we can easily move on, if and when we're ready.

In the past few years, we've been more physically active than since in our 20's. We've taken the opportunity presented by our beautiful mountain location, our unscheduled free time in retirement, and our financial independence, to catch up on a host of outdoor climbing, biking, and hiking adventures.

But the story isn't all fun and games: Last winter, we both had significant health issues. We're grateful for our solid health insurance coverage and the excellent care we received. But we are getting older, and our activity level has been taken down a notch, possibly forever. We'll still have great adventures. Life is well worth living. But there is less of it left now.

I am unceasingly grateful that I retired years ago, and took the opportunity to pursue my dreams, while I still could.

The 6 Crucial Questions

Readers and friends often ask me about the retirement decision-making "process." How do you prepare, a year out, 6 months out, 3 months out? Do you need a written plan? What about contingencies? Do you just pull the plug, or is there a more systematic way? When is it really *safe* to leave?

I'd be stretching the truth to say that I followed a meticulous, step-by-step approach to my own early retirement. Yes, there were benchmarks and milestones that I observed. There were critical tasks I knew I had to check off. But it wasn't a perfectly integrated process.

Now, in retrospect, I can see that it was all about answering a half-dozen key questions. So, here they are for your benefit in thinking through the biggest financial decision of the rest of your life....

1. How much does it cost me to live?

Go to any professional financial advisor for a retirement plan, and the first thing they're likely to hand you is a questionnaire about your living expenses. Unless you're fantastically wealthy, it's simply impossible to prepare for retirement without knowing how much it will cost you to live each month. That number will dictate the required size of your nest egg, and will figure in how you should allocate and draw down your assets.

Though it's not strictly necessary, I strongly preferred to have my major life expenses behind me before I got serious about retirement. That meant no debt of any kind. Our house had been paid off for years. But my son was partway through college. And, it wasn't until he had reached a point that I could predict his education expenses for the remaining years, that I was ready to pull the plug on my own full time career.

2. How will I get health care?

When I retired in 2011, and for many years before that, it was extremely difficult to claim your freedom before full retirement age for this simple reason: Health insurance wasn't available at reasonable cost! Unless you were one of the fortunate few who had worked for the government or a very large corporation, retiree health benefits were nonexistent. I worked in small business or as a consultant most of my professional life, and the options were grim. Fortunately, my wife had retirement health care benefits through her public school teacher position.

Now, as covered in section 1, Obamacare has changed the landscape for health care both pre- and post-retirement. But it has not perfectly simplified your choices, nor made them affordable in all cases. You'd still be well advised to explore and confirm your health care options carefully before launching into retirement and leaving your current coverage behind. And you'll have to keep one eye on the political environment, and another on the government's bottom line, to guess whether Obamacare will survive in its current form or not.

3. How much do I need to have saved?

People obsess about this number, and financial advisors are all too happy to indulge their worries with fees for sophisticated retirement plans, updated annually, that supposedly dispel all uncertainty. But, rather than taking the back seat as a passenger, passively watching events while drawing down your assets in retirement, plan instead on "driving" it using flexible income and spending levels, within sensible ranges. That is much more realistic than trying to save enough money that there is no possibility of ever running out – nearly impossible to accomplish, or even prove, for most of us.

The simple truth I've hammered home throughout this book is that *nobody can predict the future*. And the farther off that future, and the more variables involved, the less predictable it gets. The good news is that you *can* achieve enough certainty to make a decision. I did, and so have many others.

The very simple answer to this question is that you probably need a nest egg between 20-33 times the shortfall between your guaranteed income like Social Security or pensions and your annual expenses. That's between a 3% and 5% withdrawal rate. Where in that range you fall, depends on your age, your views about your future, and your lifestyle flexibility. I recommend comparing results from at least two good retirement calculators to gain more confidence. And, if your withdrawal rate will be on the high side of that range, be prepared to work again, at least part-time, if needed.

4. How will I withdraw from my savings?
The second greatest conundrum in all of retirement planning, after how much you need, is probably *how do you withdraw from it* over the years? There are nearly as many opinions, products, and services as there are pundits, academics, and financial advisors. As I explained earlier,

you can do fixed withdrawals, or variable withdrawals in several different flavors each. You can annuitize: turn the decisions, and the profits, over to an insurance company. You can, if you're fortunate, just try to preserve capital, living off interest, dividends, growth, and some part-time work.

Maybe new research and regulation will eventually produce a safe, simple, turnkey retirement income system that we can all trust. Meanwhile, the watchwords "flexible" and "dynamic" keep popping up. Turns out there may not be one, static way to live off your assets in retirement. Rather, a hybrid of existing strategies could be best. And you can't just "set and forget it." You've got to revisit your expenses, and your assets, and the state of the world, at least annually. You, or an advisor, must personally *drive* your retirement finances. You can't just put them on cruise control.

5. What will I do all day?

Most of us who have entered retirement on the early side, in good health, and with an interest in experiencing and contributing to life around us, aren't satisfied with a full-time leisure lifestyle. Yes, it is great to make your own hours, to go on vacation whenever you choose, to catch up on your bucket list and all the things you wanted to do when you were younger. I've done a lot of that. *But it only goes so far.*

The odds for long-term happiness are higher if you can identify some retirement activities that are not only fun and recreational, but also *creative*, *productive*, and *generous*. And it can be smart to test-drive those post-retirement options before you say goodbye to your career.

Some people discover their career *is* their ongoing passion in life, and they continue working. Nothing wrong with that. In fact, those people are among the most fortunate. Either way, it's best to explore your true calling, before you quit your job!

6. Do I have a backup plan?

The earlier you retire, or the higher your withdrawal rate against your savings, the more potential for dramatic financial changes that could throw you out of your retirement game plan.

What will you do if your expenses are greater than expected, if market returns are lower, if inflation is higher, if Social Security is cut? My previous discussions on *early* versus *traditional* retirement, and the expense- and income-based **lifeboat strategies**, should be your guide.

But changes to your retirement plan can also be *good*. That has been the case in my early retirement *so far*: The bull market has continued, we received a modest inheritance, and my blog has produced a bit of income. But I don't take any of this for granted. And neither should any retiree facing decades of personal, political, and economic uncertainty.

Security in retirement doesn't come from having precise numbers or an exhaustive plan for an inherently unknowable future. It comes from having the understanding and tools to navigate whatever lies ahead....

Leaving Work

So, you've answered the crucial retirement questions as best you can. You know your living expenses, and how you'll get health care. You've saved enough, and you have a strategy for withdrawing from those savings in retirement. You have a plan for how you'll spend your time, and a backup plan if there are serious financial surprises.

You're now ready to disengage and *say goodbye* to your career. How do you go about that?

Change is never easy. This is the point where you leave the numbers behind, and deal with human beings.

Most likely, you are a valued employee, or you wouldn't have reached this point of financial independence in the first place. You want to leave on the best of terms, ideally at the end of a successful project, so your organization is well positioned to deal with replacing you.

You'll remember this transition for the rest of your life, and you don't want any regrets, if possible.

You start by telling your boss, then your closest colleagues, then the others. Ideally, you'll take a hand in your succession planning, choosing and training whoever will replace you.

But, at this point, you must admit that you are no longer in control of the process. You've chosen to leave, to hand over the reins to another generation. Accept that. You've got an appointment with the rest of your life.

Finally, you say "goodbye," ideally with affection and appreciation. Then, you turn around, step forward, and launch into the next stage of your life....

Postscript: Should You Work One More Year?

My first summer in Santa Fe was the first one since my 20's that I could spend entirely in the big mountains of the west. If I was to have any regrets when that year was over, it wouldn't be because I hadn't been outdoors hiking, biking, and climbing enough....

The season began on a frosty night in May, camped beside an alpine lake in the Sangre de Cristo Mountains. And it ended in early October, gliding through neon gold aspens in Crested Butte. In between, I spent a dozen nights out on the trail, summited several 12,000-foot peaks, did a bunch of rock climbs, and logged miles of epic riding on my mountain bike.

None of that meant much, by worldly standards. But it meant a lot to me. Doing these things enriched my life, and left me with fewer regrets, should it all end tomorrow. And they wouldn't have been possible, if I were still stuck at a desk in my corporate job....

How many more seasons like that will I get? In between the fun, there are persistent reminders that I'm getting older....

Retirement Range

I'm grateful to be able to chase my remaining dreams here in middle age. I could have worked longer, accumulating more money and more security. But I was in range to retire, and I chose a different path.

And, how about you? Should you work another year, or should you pull the plug on a full-time career and take another path, before it's too late? How much longer do you have to follow your dreams?

This is a difficult, very personal decision. If you can live on 3% to 5% of your savings, you *probably* have enough to retire, if things go reasonably well. But nothing is guaranteed.

If you're within that range, but without a definite answer, what should you do? Keep trading your life's energy for more security – work another year, or make the leap to something else?

Looking in the Mirror
There is a school of thought that people are rational robots who should choose the activity that maximizes their financial value – that they shouldn't work for less than they're "worth." But that ignores quality of life....

Most of us have changing formulas for happiness over time. I loved my work in the early years, was fascinated by computers and programming, and immersed myself in the field, day and night. But, eventually, I reached the peak of what I could accomplish, and the passion faded. Other interests came to the foreground.

Twice I made major career decisions that involved turning down a management/executive track, and probable ensuing promotions and raises. These weren't the financially optimal decisions, but they improved my happiness and my quality of life. And things turned out OK on the financial front, anyway!

The reality we all face in approaching retirement is that we are closer to the end of life than the beginning. None of us knows for certain just how much longer we have left.

I ask myself the question frequently: *"If it all ends soon, am I going to be satisfied with how I've been spending my time?"*

And, beyond some simple financial calculations, I think *that* is the best way to know whether you should work one more year.

> *"...for the past 33 years, I have looked in the mirror every morning and asked myself: 'If today were the last day of my life, would I want to do what I am about to do today?' And whenever the answer has been 'No' for too many days in a row, I know I need to change something."* — Steve Jobs

Feedback

If you found this book helpful, please tell others by rating and reviewing it on amazon.com. Just describe what insights were most useful, and how they helped you. And *thank you*: I value and appreciate your support very much!

If you have any concerns, or ideas for future editions, please contact me personally. My goal is to deliver great value via simple, practical, real-world wisdom. Your feedback is essential to let me know how I'm doing. I'm always interested in hearing questions and suggestions from readers. I review every message, and reply to as many as possible.

You can reach me by email at: **darrow@caniretireyet.com**

Regards,
Darrow Kirkpatrick
CanIRetireYet.com

Acknowledgments

My financial education began with the rock-solid foundation bestowed by my parents, who taught me integrity, economy, and the value of work.

Most of my material success in life began when I met John Haestad. Thank you, John, for the opportunities, and the lessons, over so many years.

I owe an enormous debt to Richard C. Young and his *Intelligence Report* which was my mentor in patient, diversified, low-cost passive index investing.

In my new role as author and financial blogger, I have been humbled by the generosity of the personal finance community. In recent years I am particularly indebted to Mike Piper, Todd Tresidder, Mr. Money Mustache, Farnoosh Torabi, James Collins, and Penny Wang, for their support of my efforts, and my message. Special thanks to Stuart Matthews for sharing his extensive technical expertise in retirement modeling.

My editor Meghan Stevenson played a large role in the initial vision and structure for this book. Reader and friend Nicole Gabel took a keen interest in the project and provided invaluable feedback on the manuscript.

In the beginning and the end, my wife, Caroline, has enthusiastically supported and been part of this project as she has so many others before, and my son Alex has continued to encourage and inspire me. My journey, my successes, my life, are inseparable from theirs.

About the Author

Darrow Kirkpatrick is an author, software engineer, and investor who participated in several technology startups and retired at age 50. He is married to a retired schoolteacher and is the father of an amazing artist and engineer. He is an experienced rock climber and enthusiastic mountain biker, and writes regularly about saving, investing, and retiring at *CanIRetireYet.com*

His first book is *Retiring Sooner*.

Index

T

W

54671284R00153

Made in the USA
Lexington, KY
24 August 2016